Working with
Library Collections

LIBRARY SUPPORT STAFF HANDBOOKS

The Library Support Staff Handbook series is designed to meet the learning needs of both students in library support staff programs and library support staff working in libraries who want to increase their knowledge and skills.

The series was designed and is edited by Hali Keeler and Marie Shaw, both of whom teach in support staff programs and have managed libraries.

The content of each volume aligns to the competencies of the required and elective courses of the American Library Association–Allied Professional Association (ALA-APA) Library Support Staff Certification (LSSC) program. These books are both textbooks for library instructional programs and current resources for working library staff. Each book is available in both print and e-book versions.

Published books in the series include:

1. *Foundations of Library Services: An Introduction for Support Staff*
2. *Library Technology and Digital Resources: An Introduction for Support Staff*
3. *Cataloging Library Resources: An Introduction for Support Staff*
4. *Working with Library Collections: An Introduction for Support Staff*

Working with Library Collections

An Introduction for Support Staff

Hali R. Keeler

Library Support Staff Handbooks, No. 4

ROWMAN & LITTLEFIELD
Lanham • Boulder • New York • London

Published by Rowman & Littlefield
A wholly owned subsidary of The Rowman & Littlefield Publishing Group, Inc.
4501 Forbes Boulevard, Suite 200, Lanham, Maryland 20706
www.rowman.com

Unit A, Whitacre Mews, 26-34 Stannary Street, London SE11 4AB

British Library Cataloguing in Publication Information Available

Library of Congress Cataloging-in-Publication Data Available

LCCN 2016039955 | ISBN 9781442274884 (hardback : alk. paper) | 9781442274891 (pbk. : alk. paper) | ISBN 9781442274907 (electronic)

Printed in the United States of America

To library support staff—
we couldn't do it without you.

Contents

viii   *Contents*

Figures

Tables and Textboxes

Preface

Working with Collections: An Introduction for Support Staff is designed as an introduction to working with library collections. It is aligned with the *Collections* competencies as determined by the Library Support Staff Certification (LSSC) Program of the American Library Association (ALA).

Each chapter begins with the LSSC Competencies that are to be addressed, followed by a list of topics that will be covered, as well as a glossary of key terms. Chapters are then broken into easily readable sections that relate back to these key terms. Figures, tables, and photographs are included to highlight concepts and set them apart for emphasis. The language is uncomplicated but appropriate to the material being covered. Actual library experiences are included to illustrate how these concepts work in the real world. Each chapter concludes with a summary plus questions and opportunities for extensions of learning. Readers of this text will come away with a basic knowledge of working with collections in a library.

Library support staff (LSS) are known by many names and have various levels of responsibilities. They may hold such titles as library assistants, library technical assistants, library associates, or library aides. This book can serve as a reference or refresher for them; it meets the needs of the student in a library certificate or degree program; and it can serve as a text for an instructor in such a program. This is the audience for which the book is intended.

The book contains clear wording and ample definitions, and many figures, tables, and photos help illustrate the concepts that are presented. Additionally, end-of-chapter summaries, review questions and activities, and a section of "References, Suggested Readings, and Websites" provides access to supplementary resources that will provide further support for instructors or to meet the individual interests of the student or the library worker.

The scope of *Working with Collections: An Introduction for Support Staff* assures that the reader will learn in detail about working with collections in three discrete sections. In Part I: Collections, LSS receive an overview of collections and collection development, including commonly used terminology. It covers the mission of each kind of library—public, academic, school, and special—and describes how the mission relates to the collection of materials in each. Also covered are the elements of the collection as well as an assessment of the community and its needs. Selection and acquisition of materials in all formats are explained, as is the management of the collection, inventory of the collection, and ultimately the deselection of items. Coverage is given to the many options for dealing with deselected materials. Part II: Tools and Technology introduces the reader to the Integrated Library System (ILS) and its modules, as well as databases and networks and their role in the collection process. Networks and the cooperative systems that link libraries are also considered for their role. The importance of collection statistics and use is covered in determining collection strengths and weaknesses. The use of statistics in creating local and state reports is a valuable inclusion, as is their use in library planning and budgets. Part III: Collection Care gives readers valuable guidance in basic materials repair, the preservation of items as well as entire collections, and very practical instructions for preparing materials in all formats for circulation and use in the library.

Working with Collections: An Introduction for Support Staff breaks new ground, as it is written expressly to align with the competencies required by the American Library Association Library Support Staff Certification Program. The author's experience teaching in a library technology program, as well as extensive research, has shown that there is a lack of appropriate instructional materials for the non-MLS student. Texts on the market are geared for the graduate level and as such are often too theoretical and technical for this level of study. The Library Support Staff Series is meant to meet this need and to provide a resource and reference for those already working in the field.

This book's features will be useful to LSS in building and improving their skills and knowledge of working with collections. Textboxes provide visual emphasis on particular techniques and concepts that are important to know. Figures and photographs reinforce the step-by-step instructions and practical information. The many tables are useful resources the LSS can rely on to guide them or use as checklists as they experience these scenarios in the real world. Additionally, the chapter questions and activities provide opportunities for the LSS to review what they have learned to practice in the workplace. This book is intended to be a guide to the actual day-to-day activities that LSS will encounter.

Working with Collections: An Introduction for Support Staff came about after years of teaching LSS courses using textbooks that were designed for graduate-level study. While those books were full of good information, the students often found it difficult to wade through technical, theoretical, and complex content they would not use as support staff. Content for this book was then developed out of the author's thirty-five years of experience as a children's librarian, library director, and adjunct professor in an LSSC-certified program and was designed to align with the ALA LSSC Competencies. The current literature, research, and hands-on practice all contributed to the content, as did the author's instructional experience with courses at Three Rivers Community College on library public services, library technical services, and management strategies.

Use of this text will give the LSS the tools, skills, and basic knowledge that they need to work at a variety of collection activities in a library of any kind. Depending on the size and staff needs of the library, the LSS will be able to assist with all phases of the process, including covering new books, circulating materials properly to avoid damage, caring for and housing all formats, performing basic material repair, and ultimately seeing to the conservation of the entire collection.

While designed as a textbook, *Working with Collections: An Introduction for Support Staff* is equally valuable for those who already work in a library. They will find it a handy reference and support in their work, as it will give them supplemental information that they may lack or serve to reinforce their existing skills.

Acknowledgments

There are several people I would like to thank for their efforts on my behalf:

- My sincere thanks go to my colleague, Marie Shaw, for her support, advice, and friendship. Your help continues to be invaluable and most appreciated. The journey continues.
- I am indebted to my publisher, Charles Harmon, for his encouragement, support, and patience.
- With appreciation to the Editorial Advisory Board for their professional appraisals, keen eyes, and suggestions—but mostly for taking the time out of their busy schedules to consult on this book.
- With love and thanks to my husband, Gerry, for his support, encouragement, and technical expertise.

Editorial Advisory Board

PART I

Collections

CHAPTER 1

Library Collections Today

Library Support Staff (LSS) know the basic principles of collection development and man-agement, and the principles and procedures to the processes that provide content to users. (ALA-LSSC Competencies #2 and #4)

Topics Covered in This Chapter:

- Collection Development Overview
  - Library Missions
  - Elements of Collection
- Community Assessment
- Needs Assessment

Key Terms:

Acquisitions: Acquisitions is the function of collections that concerns ordering and receiv-ing print and nonprint materials. Specifically, the acquisitions department, or the LSS who work in acquisitions, uses evaluative sources to find and verify that an item exists, chooses a vendor, places the order, maintains a fiscal record, and receives the materials.

Cataloging: Cataloging means creating a bibliographic record of an item. In addition, we use numerical or alphabetical classification systems to organize materials by subject. These systems provide for the arrangement of materials on a shelf or in a database in logical order, making it easy for patrons to find that for which they are searching. This is an important factor in creating collections.

Collection: A collection can have many meanings but is usually thought of as a group of objects or materials accumulated in one place, usually for some purpose. In the library setting it is an accumulation of information resources in multiple formats, usually developed by library professionals for a particular group of users. These materials are usually connected to each other in some way as well as connected to an intended audience, or user.

Collection policy: A collection policy is a document that provides guidance for the librarians or LSS who do collection development. It follows a set of guidelines to consider when choosing materials, and includes such criteria as positive reviews, reputation of the author, local interest, demand, and budget limitations.

Community assessment: Community assessment is the analysis of the demographics of a community. Statistical data is a good place to start to determine the population, age range, genders, and ethnicities of a particular area, as well as employers, types of households, age, number of schools and libraries, social service providers, languages spoken, and median family incomes.

Demographics: Demographics are the statistics of a given population by age, sex, race, and income. This is important for libraries so they can know whom they are serving, and for whom they can provide the appropriate resources. This is a key component of community assessment and subsequently, collection development.

Mission: An organization's mission identifies its value and purpose to the community it serves. It explains what the organization is, and what functions it serves. By establishing a mission, usually in a "mission statement," an organization or library can develop and provide the services that meet the needs of their constituents.

Needs assessment: A needs assessment is a systematic process for determining and addressing needs, or "gaps" between current conditions and desired "wants." The discrepancy between the current condition and wanted condition must be measured to appropriately identify the need.[1]

Preparation: Preparation means making print and nonprint items ready for use, such as the physical processing of items. The LSS must use methods to establish ownership of the library's materials, and provide for its tracking once it goes into the collection.

Selection/deselection: Selection means choosing the materials that a library will purchase using such tools as review journals, online programs, electronic databases, vendors, and "best lists." Selection must take into account the demographics of the library's community as well as the funds available. Deselection involves removing materials from the collection due to age, condition, and outdated information, among other considerations.

Storage: Storage, an integral part of collection management, includes the routine and appropriate shelving of materials according to their format. It also involves shelf reading to determine that the collection is in order; collection shifting to allow for the accommodation of the addition or withdrawal of materials, as well as print and digital management.

COLLECTION DEVELOPMENT OVERVIEW

Library Missions

Like most nonprofit organizations, libraries have **missions**. They are usually expressed in the form of a mission statement to define "who we are and what we do."[2] Often combined with a vision statement, it identifies the value and purpose of a library. A mission statement should be short, clear, and powerful. Similarly a vision statement defines your organization's purpose, but focuses on what it wants to achieve over time. Common elements in library mission statements include such terms as "lifelong learning," "building communities," "connecting people and information," and "commitment to literacy." This informs everything that a library does—most particularly, its collection. An example of a generic public library mission statement might look like this:

TEXTBOX 1.1 SAMPLE PUBLIC LIBRARY MISSION STATEMENT

The mission of the Anytown Public Library is to connect people to the transforming power of knowledge, to enrich lives, and to strengthen our community.

TEXTBOX 1.2 SAMPLE SCHOOL LIBRARY MISSION STATEMENT

The mission of the Anytown School Library is to provide activities and resources that will assist students in becoming critical thinkers, enthusiastic readers, skillful researchers, and informed users of information.

These same concepts hold true for academic libraries with the addition of words such as "supports curriculum," "promotes access," "prepares students for the changing workplace," and "facilitates learning"—as well as language that supports the mission of the college or university.

TEXTBOX 1.3 SAMPLE ACADEMIC LIBRARY MISSION STATEMENT

The mission of Anystate College Library is to serve as an intellectual and knowledge center as well as provide access and support curriculum for its students, faculty, and staff. It supports curriculum, promotes access, facilitates learning, and contributes to information literacy while seeking to improve institutional outcomes.

Finally there is the specialized library, which would be found at a corporation, museum, hospital, church, or prison, for example. Special libraries are designed to support the organization for which they were created and by which they are funded and as such, must prove their value to the organization.

TEXTBOX 1.4 SAMPLE SPECIALIZED LIBRARY MISSION STATEMENT

The mission of the Anytown Art Museum Library is to develop collections and serve as a cultural resource center to connect people to exhibitions, publications, educational initiatives, and programs, and to support institutional outcomes.

Elements of Collection

Let's begin by determining what a **collection** is. The term can have many meanings but is usually thought of as a group of objects or materials accumulated in one place, usually for some purpose.[3] People collect all sorts of things, from baseball cards to garden gnomes. In the library setting, however, it is an accumulation of information resources in multiple formats, developed by library professionals for a particular group of users. These materials are usually connected to each other in some way as well as connected to an intended audience, or user.[4] The items in a library collection can be physical, like a book or CD, or digital, as in a journal article in a database or an electronic book downloadable to a device.

In a library, collection development consists of the **selection** of materials that the librarian believes will be useful to the community. A librarian would follow a set of guidelines that would include adhering to the institution's **collection policy** and using standard review sources to find and evaluate materials. The **acquisitions** process would be the next stage, including bibliographically identifying each item as well as the sources of purchase.

Once materials are ordered and delivered, the staff then has to organize or **catalog** the materials so they can be easily located within the library. Before they can circulate, however, the materials have to be **prepared**, or physically processed. Finally, and probably most importantly, the source of funds must be identified from which these purchases can be made. For this, the library must have a budget that will include the purchase of books and materials as well as different kinds of supplies, maintenance, salaries, and so on.

When books and other materials are placed on the shelf they must be maintained; their **storage** and eventual disposition is an ongoing task that includes shelving (putting items back on the shelf after use), shelf reading (assuring that everything on the shelf is in order), and shifting the items if the shelving is too tight. Finally, books and other items must eventually be "weeded," or **deselected** from the collection to make room for newer titles.

There are other ways to add to a collection besides purchasing materials. Often the cost of an individual item must be considered, as well as the subject matter of the area of the collection into which it will fall.[5] The use of interlibrary loan can bring in specific titles or items that the library cannot afford to purchase or that they may need extra copies of for a book group or project. Many states have a library service center (sort of a library for libraries), where materials can be borrowed in bulk to temporarily augment the collection, particularly in subject areas of demand or specialized items such as current large-type books, Playaways, books on CD, or materials to support a local school project.

Elements of the above will be discussed in detail in subsequent chapters.

COMMUNITY ASSESSMENT

Those who work in collection development (and for that matter everyone who works in a particular library) must know the library's demographic. **Demographics** are the statistics of a given population by age, sex, race, and income.[6] One must assess the community in which the library is located in order to determine who lives there and what their needs might be. This can be done by hiring consultants to do in-depth statistical studies—or it can be done as informally as walking down the street.

Technically, the service area for a public library is the town that provides its funding. School or academic libraries would find their service area, or demographic, to be the students attending that school or college—which could consist of a variety of ages, ethnicities, and income levels. Academic libraries also have to consider the teaching faculty in their demographic, as their collections need to include materials to support faculty research.

Not everyone within the boundaries of your town will be library users. On the other hand, many people enjoy visiting libraries in their own, or surrounding, towns. Still others will visit your library without leaving home by accessing your resources online. Someone who lives in another town but works in the same town as your library may also become a regular patron. For example, say a town is home to several large industries that draw its workers from all over the area. Some of the library's most loyal patrons can live almost an hour away, but because this library is on their way to and from work, it becomes "their" library. People can get very attached to libraries, regardless of location. The permeability of a town's borders can increase your service area considerably, and thus affect your collection objectives. Interlibrary loan and digital content provide access to a far wider population as well.

In conducting a formal community assessment there are a number of factors to consider. Statistical data is a good place to start to determine the population, age range, genders, and ethnicities of a particular area. A community assessment can be done in-house by using an analysis survey tool. One example of this is the Community Analysis Scan Form produced by the Colorado State Library.[7] It includes such fields as Census Bureau maps, employers, types of households, age, number of schools and libraries, social service providers, languages spoken, and median family incomes.

It can also be done fairly simply by using census information accessible from the government at American Fact Finder.[8] By submitting the desired zip code, town, or state, one can choose population, age, business and industry, education, housing, income, languages, and several other categories. It offers a granular search with the availability of detailed breakdowns, such as occupation by sex and median earnings by selected year. Since the U.S. Census is only conducted and updated every ten years, the information will necessarily be somewhat out of date, although the site does provide updated information by estimate for succeeding years. The following charts represent two examples created from American Fact Finder Community Facts. The first one is for a small town with one zip code.

The second chart is representative of a very large city of multiple zip codes included in one chart. This city has a multi-branch library system; a further breakdown by zip code might show different results, which would influence collection development for each branch.

Table 1.1. Sample Community Facts for a Small Town

Description	Measure	Source
Population		
Census 2010 total population	31,242	2010 Demographic Profile
2014 population estimate (as of July 1, 2014)	N/A	2014 Population Estimates
2013 ACS 5-year population estimate	31,769	2009–2013 American Community Survey 5-Year Estimates
Median age	30.5	2009–2013 American Community Survey 5-Year Estimates
Number of companies	N/A	2007 Survey of Business Owners
Educational attainment: percent high school graduate or higher	90.9%	2009–2013 American Community Survey 5-Year Estimates
Count of governments	N/A	2012 Census of Governments
Total housing units	14,137	2009–2013 American Community Survey 5-Year Estimates
Median household income	55,992	2009–2013 American Community Survey 5-Year Estimates
Foreign-born population	2,486	2009–2013 American Community Survey 5-Year Estimates
Individuals below poverty level	10.0%	2009–2013 American Community Survey 5-Year Estimates
Race and Hispanic Origin		
White alone	24,438	2009–2013 American Community Survey 5-Year Estimates
Black or African American alone	2,108	2009–2013 American Community Survey 5-Year Estimates
American Indian and Alaska Native alone	202	2009–2013 American Community Survey 5-Year Estimates
Asian alone	1,688	2009–2013 American Community Survey 5-Year Estimates
Native Hawaiian and other Pacific Islander alone	57	2009–2013 American Community Survey 5-Year Estimates
Some other race alone	1,016	2009–2013 American Community Survey 5-Year Estimates
Two or more races	2,260	2009–2013 American Community Survey 5-Year Estimates
Hispanic or Latino (of any race)	3,717	2009–2013 American Community Survey 5-Year Estimates
White alone, not Hispanic or Latino	22,313	2009–2013 American Community Survey 5-Year Estimates
Veterans	2,826	2009–2013 American Community Survey 5-Year Estimates

Table 1.2. Sample Community Facts Large City

Description	Measure	Source
Population		
Census 2010 total population	608,660	2010 Demographic Profile
2014 population estimate (as of July 1, 2014)	668,342	2014 Population Estimates
2013 ACS 5-year population estimate	624,681	2009–2013 American Community Survey 5-Year Estimates
Median age	36.1	2009–2013 American Community Survey 5-Year Estimates
Number of companies	73,997	2007 Survey of Business Owners
Educational attainment: percent high school graduate or higher	93.2%	2009–2013 American Community Survey 5-Year Estimates
Count of governments	N/A	2012 Census of Governments
Total housing units	309,205	2009–2013 American Community Survey 5-Year Estimates
Median household income	65,277	2009–2013 American Community Survey 5-Year Estimates
Foreign-born population	110,496	2009–2013 American Community Survey 5-Year Estimates
Individuals below poverty level	13.6%	2009–2013 American Community Survey 5-Year Estimates
Race and Hispanic origin		
White alone	440,866	2009–2013 American Community Survey 5-Year Estimates
Black or African American alone	46,310	2009–2013 American Community Survey 5-Year Estimates
American Indian and Alaska Native alone	4,474	2009–2013 American Community Survey 5-Year Estimates
Asian alone	87,953	2009–2013 American Community Survey 5-Year Estimates
Native Hawaiian and other Pacific Islander alone	2,567	2009–2013 American Community Survey 5-Year Estimates
Some other race alone	9,791	2009–2013 American Community Survey 5-Year Estimates
Two or more races	32,720	2009–2013 American Community Survey 5-Year Estimates
Hispanic or Latino (of any race)	40,110	2009–2013 American Community Survey 5-Year Estimates
White alone, not Hispanic or Latino	416,569	2009–2013 American Community Survey 5-Year Estimates
Veterans	32,864	2009–2013 American Community Survey 5-Year Estimates

Those are the statistics. Observing who is actually using the library, taking informal surveys, conducting focus groups, or simply talking to and interacting with patrons can also give a pretty good idea of a library's demographic, including children, older adults, or languages spoken. In a typical library of any type there will be a mix of races and ethnicities whose needs must be addressed when choosing materials. If yours is an urban library it is likely to serve a more diverse population. The upshot is that a community assessment, no matter how formally or informally it is conducted, will provide the needed information to inform the collection development of that library.

Having such information about the median age, income, and education (among other statistics) of your community helps to determine who your patrons are. Building on that allows for collection development to be more specifically targeted to those patrons.

NEEDS ASSESSMENT

Closely related to community assessment is **needs assessment**. Once the community assessment is done, the results are used to plan for the needs of the patrons that have been identified. This necessitates a *needs assessment* of the population. "With patron and community needs always evolving and expanding, how do we know we're providing the right services? When funders ask questions we can't answer, how do we gather evidence of the library's importance?"[9]

A needs assessment begins by determining what you already know about your library's needs, whether it's for additional resources or new technologies—and what library doesn't always need more money and newer technology? This helps to better understand the gaps (needs) between where you are and where you want to be. Data can be collected from library statistics or records, or through surveys and the analysis of statistical data that may have been collected during the community assessment. After the data is collected, it is organized and analyzed to create a plan of action for such things as strategic planning, determining changes in the user community, making changes in a library's collection and services, determining the adequacy of facilities and technology, and establishing satisfactory staffing patterns and library hours.

For example, the community assessment may show that the library's target area has a larger immigrant population than it did five years ago. The gap, or need, then is to figure out how to better serve this community. The data may show that the library does not have up-to-date materials and resources in the languages of this population; therefore the plan of action would be to find the funds to purchase these materials. The library would then advertise this service through marketing, outreach, and community partnerships.

A needs assessment process reveals the influences acting on the library. The information collected shapes the services and programs that best fit the library's strengths and budget. Ultimately, it informs a vision for future development.[10]

CHAPTER SUMMARY

This chapter provides an overview of the collection development process, including library missions and elements of collection. It presents the concept of community and needs assessments to determine a particular library's demographic, which is critical to collection development so that the right material makes it to the right patron.

DISCUSSION QUESTIONS

1. Find the mission statements of three different libraries. How are they similar and how are they different?
2. Describe the elements of collection development.
3. Explain what is meant by "demographics." How is it relevant to collection development?
4. How might a library prioritize needs based on their community assessment? What factors should be considered?
5. Explain the principles of selection and deselection.

ACTIVITIES

1. Collect sample policies on acquiring and making library resources available to users from three different libraries of varying type and size. Compare and contrast these policies. What aspects of each do you think are best and why?
2. Perform a community analysis of your town to determine who your library users might be. What methods will you use, and what is the outcome?

NOTES

1. "What Is Needs Assessment?," video file, Study.com, accessed April 6, 2016, http://study.com/academy/lesson/what-is-needs-assessment-definition-examples-quiz.html.

2. Joseph R. Matthews, *Strategic Planning and Management for Library Managers* (Westport, CT: Libraries Unlimited, 2005), 14.

3. "Collection," Dictionary.com, accessed November 14, 2015, http://dictionary.reference.com/browse/collection.

4. Wayne Disher, *Collection Development*, Crash Course Series (Westport, CT: Libraries Unlimited, 2014), 1–2.

5. Kathleen A. Layman, "Collection Development and Management: An Overview of the Literature, 2011–12," *Library Resources & Technical Services*, April 10, 2014, 171.

6. "Business Data and Statistics: Demographics," U.S. Small Business Association, accessed November 13, 2015, https://www.sba.gov/content/demographics.

7. "Community Analysis Scan Form," Library Research Service, accessed November 12, 2015, http://www.lrs.org/public/ca_form.php.

8. United States Census Bureau, "Community Facts," *American Fact Finder*, http://factfinder.census.gov/faces/nav/jsf/pages/index.xhtml.

9. "Explore Topics: Needs Assessment," *Webjunction,* last modified 2016, accessed April 6, 2016, https://www.webjunction.org/explore-topics/needs-assessment.html.

10. "Needs Assessment," Idaho Commission for Libraries, accessed April 6, 2016, http://libraries.idaho.gov/page/needs-assessment.

REFERENCES, SUGGESTED READINGS, AND WEBSITES

American Library Association. "ALA's Core Competences of Librarianship." American Library Association. Last modified January 27, 2009. Accessed October 5, 2015. http://www.ala.org/educationcareers/sites/ala.org.educationcareers/files/content/careers/corecomp/corecompetences/finalcorecompstat09.pdf.

Bass, Hayden, CiKeithia Pugh, and Rekha Kuver. "Community Engagement: Serving Diverse Communities Where They Are." *Webjunction.* Last modified January 28, 2016. Accessed April 6, 2016. http://www.webjunction.org/events/webjunction/community-engagement-serving-diverse-communities-where-they-are.html.

————. "Library Support Staff Certification." American Library Association–Allied Professional Association (ALA-APA). Accessed November 16, 2015. http://ala-apa.org/lssc/.

Bureau of Labor Statistics. "Library Technicians and Assistants." *Occupational Outlook Handbook.* Accessed October 5, 2015. http://www.bls.gov/ooh/education-training-and-library/library-technicians-and-assistants.htm.

Colorado State Library. "Community Analysis Scan Form." Library Research Service. Accessed November 12, 2015. http://www.lrs.org/public/ca_form.php.

Dictionary.com. "Collection." Dictionary.com. Accessed November 14, 2015. http://dictionary.reference.com/browse/collection.

Disher, Wayne. *Collection Development.* Crash Course Series. Westport, CT: Libraries Unlimited, 2014.

Evans, G. Edward, Sheila S. Intner, and Jean Weihs. *Introduction to Technical Services.* 8th ed. Library and Information Science Text Series. Santa Barbara, CA: Libraries Unlimited, 2011.

Idaho Commission for Libraries. "Needs Assessment." Idaho Commission for Libraries. Accessed April 6, 2016. http://libraries.idaho.gov/page/needs-assessment.

Layman, Kathleen A. "Collection Development and Management: An Overview of the Literature, 2011–12." *Library Resources & Technical Services,* April 10, 2014, 169–77.

OCLC. "Library Staff Competencies Collection." *Webjunction.* Last modified March 21, 2012. Accessed October 5, 2015. https://www.webjunction.org/documents/webjunction/Library_Staff_Competency_Collections.html.

U.S. Census Bureau. "Community Facts." *American Fact Finder.* Accessed November 16, 2015. http://factfinder.census.gov/faces/nav/jsf/pages/index.xhtml.

U.S. Small Business Association. "Business Data and Statistics: Demographics." Accessed November 13, 2015. https://www.sba.gov/content/demographics.

"What Is Needs Assessment?" Video file. Study.com. Accessed April 6, 2016. http://study.com/academy/lesson/what-is-needs-assessment-definition-examples-quiz.html.

CHAPTER 2

Collection Development

Library Support Staff (LSS) know the basic principles of collection development and man-agement, and can explain and apply policies regarding library collections. (ALA-LSSC Competencies #2 and #10)

Topics Covered in This Chapter:

- Library Collection Development
  - Collection Analysis
- Policies
  - Academic Libraries
  - Public Libraries
  - School Libraries
    - Common Core Standards
    - Developmental Reading Assessments and Lexile Measures
- Library Funding
  - Budgets

Key Terms:

Academic library: Academic libraries serve society's need for education for those beyond high school, including community colleges, four-year colleges, and universities. Their collections serve the students and faculty of the institution. These libraries serve the teaching needs of the institution as well as the needs of the students. They may also support faculty research.

Budgets: A budget is an estimate of income and expenses over a defined period of time—usually the library's fiscal year. It is critical for libraries to keep a budget in order to determine where funds are needed for allocation, and the source from which they will come.

Collection development: Collection development refers to the process of building a library collection in a variety of formats to serve recreational, study, teaching, research, and other needs of library users. The process includes selection and deselection of materials, the planning of strategies for continuing acquisition, and evaluation of collections to determine how well they serve user needs. It includes library operations ranging from the selection of individual titles for purchase, to the withdrawal of expendable materials.

Collection policy: A collection policy, also known as a selection policy, is a document that provides guidance for the librarians or LSS who do collection development. It follows a set of guidelines to consider when choosing materials and includes such criteria as positive reviews, reputation of the author, local interest, demand, and budget limitations.

Common Core standards: The Common Core is a set of high-quality academic standards in mathematics and English Language Arts/Literacy (ELA) that help determine what a student should know and be able to do at the end of each grade. It impacts libraries and changes the way traditional library skills are being taught; it also encourages a close collaboration between school and public librarians.

Funding: Funding is the means by which libraries pay their bills. Most school and public libraries are financially supported by their local municipality; academic library funding will depend on whether it's a public or private institution. Public libraries in particular depend also on grants, donations, or fund-raising drives to augment their funds.

Integrated library systems: An integrated library system, or ILS, is a computer system and programs that link library operations.[1] It consists of components, or modules, that do different tasks. These modules are for acquisitions, cataloging, serials, and circulating materials.

Public library: The public library serves a culturally diverse population and a variety of ages, and is the most heterogeneous of any type of library. Public service then is structured around these populations to best serve their particular demographic. They are places of cultural preservation of information in its various formats and are often the hub of their community.

School library/media center: School libraries, or media centers, have evolved from a simple collection of books into a resource center of media and technology; their collections reflect the demographics of the student body. The media specialist or LSS provide library instruction and work with teachers to coordinate lesson plans and materials for classroom support.

LIBRARY COLLECTION DEVELOPMENT

The objective of any library is to serve the information needs of its users. As noted in chapter 1, who these users are will depend on the library's demographics—the statistics of a given population by age, sex, race, and income. This is important for libraries so they can know who their patrons are and provide the appropriate resources. This is a key component of **collection development**. In library terms, we use these characteristics to tailor the information to those users' needs.

Collection Analysis

The first step in collection development is to analyze the current collection. Collection analysis helps to determine what patrons are using. Although there are commercial tools available to do this (such as OCLC's collection analysis service), it can be done fairly simply through the library's integrated library system (ILS) by running reports on use by subject, areas of heaviest circulation, and so on. This can guide LSS in determining the quality of a library's collection. "Currency, turn-over rates, and other statistical data can provide clues as to the quality of the collection, as well. The central concept in the process of analyzing a collection is that collections are created, developed, and maintained to meet the needs of the community they serve. This means that the collection must remain relevant and useful to the people who are using it. Therefore, collection evaluation must also include an analysis of how well the materials are currently meeting needs and how likely the materials (and the collection) are to continue meeting the needs of current and future users."[2]

The purpose, then, of collection development is to select materials that serve the needs of the primary service population, or demographic.[3] Additionally it also contains information on weeding (or deselection), and material retention, preservation and archiving, as well as the library's mission and goals. It should also contain the process for handling complaints and the reconsideration of materials.

POLICIES

As in other areas of librarianship, a formal written policy needs to be in place to guide collection development. A **collection development policy** follows a set of guidelines to consider when choosing materials. The American Library Association defines collection development policies (CDP) as "documents which define the scope of a library's existing collections, plan for the continuing development of resources, identify collection strengths, and outline the relationship between selection philosophy and the institution's goals, general selection criteria, and intellectual freedom."[4] Also, according to the ALA,

> Policies have several functions in today's complex organizations. The very act of writing and approving them helps define the values of the organization, and once written, they help managers and the staff to translate those values into service priorities. Policies establish a standard for services that can be understood by both users of the services and providers of the service. Policies ensure equitable treatment for all, and polices provide a framework for delivery of services. When policies have been adopted by a library's governing agents in a formal process and are consistent with local, state, and federal laws, they will be enforceable.[5]

While there are a number of elements that a policy *should* contain, collection development policies may vary by institution and patron base and will be geared toward a specific community. For any type of library, elements of selection or collection development policy *may* include the following:

TEXTBOX 2.1 SAMPLE COLLECTION POLICY ELEMENTS

- Library mission statement
- Purpose of policy
- Intellectual Freedom Statement
- Collection development objectives
- Responsibility
- Gifts
- Withdrawals
- Challenged materials
- Reconsideration
- Confidentiality of circulation records
- Freedom to Read Statement
- Library Bill of Rights

In addition, it should include:

- A statement regarding who has the authority to select
- A statement regarding who is responsible for selection
- A statement regarding the library's goals and objectives
- A list of criteria for selection
- A list of review sources used
- A procedure for handling problems
- Guidelines for allocating funds
- A procedure for handling problems
- Guidelines for allocating funds

Any given policy may also have guidelines on the inclusion and selection of nonbook formats including books on CD, MP3, or Playaways; music CDs; DVDs, Blu-Ray, and emerging technologies like Archival Disc (optical discs with increased storage capacity); high resolution audio; electronic resources; and databases.

One thing that libraries agree on is the inclusion in the CDP of the Library Bill of Rights and the Freedom to Read Statement provided by the American Library Association. The Library Bill of Rights "affirms that all libraries are forums for information and ideas" and that materials "should be provided for the interest, information, and enlightenment of all people of the community the library serves. . . . [Furthermore,] materials should not be excluded because of the origin, background, or views of those contributing to their creation."[6] It also states that libraries must oppose censorship and resist the abridgment of freedom of expression. The Freedom to Read Statement tells us that this freedom to read, and to communicate, is essential to our democracy and that its suppression is counter to it. "By the exercise of this affirmative responsibility, they [librarians and publishers] can demonstrate that the answer to a 'bad' book is a good one, the answer to a 'bad' idea is a good one."[7]

Academic Libraries

Let's begin with a look at **academic library** policies. The basic criteria of a CDP will apply to the academic library collection, but it, too, has to take into consideration criteria applicable to that institution. The collection will make available to faculty and students a selection of materials that will enrich and support the curriculum and meet the needs of the students and faculty served. In universities that would also mean supporting the research and publications of faculty.

Large colleges and universities may have multiple libraries to support the various schools within the college, such as a library devoted to engineering, art, music, and so forth. Each of those libraries will have a CDP geared toward that curriculum, while still maintaining the basic tenets of overall collection development policies.

Public Libraries

There are no national laws governing **public libraries**, so each state and city is on its own to develop a collection policy for their public libraries. A CDP for a public library will be a document written by professional library staff in conjunction with, or the approval of, the library's governing authority—usually a library board of trustees. There are, however, professional associations that provide guidance, professional development, and support. On the national level there is the American Library Association and its divisions, such as the Public Library Association, Library Leadership and Management Association, or the Reference and Users Services Association. Further, each state has its own library association (e.g., CLA, the Connecticut Library Association; NJLA, the New Jersey Library Association; WLA, the Washington Library Association) that can assist. The CDP for a public library follows the same pattern described previously and may include the same elements that we've already seen. The state library (of your state) should be consulted for examples of what is acceptable or legal for that state.

The public library is typically known as "the people's university," as it is a free resource for anyone to pursue their quest for knowledge regardless of age, skill level, or economic status. The public library offers a vast array of books, magazines, newspapers, databases, and more, and is open to all. It serves culturally diverse populations of all ages. The services in the public library are thus structured around their service populations, which are generally the most heterogeneous population of any library type.

School Libraries

There is no national policy that governs how public schools regulate library collection development, so it is up to each state to establish an agency to provide public education for K–12. This is done through the department of education of each state. It is through these agencies that standards of accreditation are determined. While the states have responsibility for primary and secondary education, it is the local school districts that direct the curriculum and fund the libraries, usually via the local board of education.

As each school district or system develops its own board policies, the basic criteria of a CDP will apply to **school libraries**/media centers. One school district may be very specific about its library collection development, while another school district may be less so. ALA suggests:

> Every school system should have a comprehensive policy on the selection of instructional materials. It should relate to and include all materials; for example, textbooks, library books and materials, and all supplementary resources. . . . A good policy on the selection of instructional materials will be relevant to your particular system and include basic sections on objectives, responsibility, criteria, procedures for selection, reconsideration of materials, and policies on controversial materials.[8]

For materials in the library media center, the goals may include meeting individual learning needs, abilities, and learning styles, including for children for whom English is not their native language; providing background materials to supplement classroom instruction; and providing a broad range of materials on controversial issues to help students develop critical analytical skills.

However, other criteria applicable to both a school library and the children's collection in a public library must be taken into consideration. One of these is the **Common Core**, a set of high-quality academic standards in mathematics and English Language Arts/Literacy (ELA). These learning goals outline what a student should know and be able to do at the end of each grade.[9] (It is important to note that the concept of Common Core has not been universally accepted, and not all states have adopted it. It remains a controversial topic and its future has yet to be determined.)

Christopher Harris, librarian and director of the School Library System for the Genesee Valley Educational Partnership in Western New York, and one of its proponents writes,

> [Common Core] impacts libraries and changes the way traditional library skills are being taught; it also encourages a close collaboration between school and public librarians. Common Core calls for shorter, well-crafted texts that kids can consider more deeply. . . . Common Core is a great boon for school libraries, especially since they're a school's number-one source for the primary-source informational texts that kids need. . . . While school libraries will continue to be a source for narrative books for students, your collection development energies need to be spent on building up literary *nonfiction* resources.[10]

A number of publishers have been working with educators to get a clearer understanding of Common Core and are aligning their books accordingly. Some, such as Peachtree, Random House, and Scholastic, are creating websites, social media, and tip sheets to emphasize the standards. Still others, such as Penguin and Enslow, are creating Common Core–specific books. Most publishers feel that they have been using these standards all along, before it was given a name. According to Victoria Stapleton, director of School and Library Marketing at Little Brown for Young Readers, "Helping booksellers and librarians understand how a book can be used to fit Common Core standards can be as simple as an editor noting in the tip sheet that a novel is historical or has multiple points of view."[11]

Yet another consideration for collection development for school libraries, and public library children's rooms, is identifying materials that meet the reading needs of children at different stages in their brain development. This involves the use of various assessment tools to determine at what level a child is reading, and then having materials available that are challenging enough for that child. Among these tools are the guided reading level (GRL), the Developmental Reading Assessment (DRA) level, and Lexile measures.

The GRL is determined by having the child and the teacher work together one on one while the child reads from a story deemed to be standard for her grade. The teacher may then ask questions about the story. Depending on the results, the child will then be assigned to a small group who are at the same level where they learn to process a variety of increasingly challenging materials. Using this method rates books from A to Z, with A being the easiest.

Table 2.1. Leveled Reading Chart

Grade Level	Guided Reading Level	Lexile Level	DRA Levels
Kindergarten	A		A-1
	B		2,3
	C		4
	D		6
Grade 1	E		8
	F		10
	G	190L–530L	12
	H		14
	I		16
	J		18
Grade 2	K	420L–620L	20
	L		24
	M		28
Grade 3	N		30
	O	520L–820L	34
	P		38
Grade 4	Q		
	R	740L–940L	40
	S		
Grade 5	T		
	U	830L–1010L	50
	V		
Grade 6	W		
	X	925L–1070L	60
	Y		
Grade 7		970L–1120L	70
Grade 8	Z	1010L–1185L	80
Grade 9		1050L–1260L	
Grade 10	Z+	1080L–1335L	
Grade 11			
Grade 12		1185L–1385L	

Developmental Reading Assessment, or DRA, levels are similar to GRL in that the child will read a story to a teacher and then retell it in his or her own words. The children are then scored on a variety of factors, including accuracy, comprehension, and fluency. Like GRL, DRA begins with A as the easiest but then switches to numerical levels from 1–80.

Finally, Lexile measures are based on a school-administered Scholastic Reading Inventory (SRI) assessment. A Lexile is a measuring tool used to match readers with materials. This is designed to generate a Lexile measure of reading ability using quantitative methods based on words and sentence length. A child can also take a standardized leveled reading test that converts the results to a Lexile measure. Lexile also evaluates books for difficulty, with levels ranging from 200L to 1700L+ for advanced readers.[12] Some library databases provide magazine and journal articles with a Lexile Rating as well.

You may be wondering what this has to do with collection development policies. As we read in chapter 1, policies are informed by the library's primary service population, or demographic. In a school library, or the children's department of a public library, it is necessary to be able to provide materials for the reading levels and interests of all ages and abilities. Both Common Core Standards and guided reading levels will ensure that the collection is developed to meet the needs of all students.

Figure 2.1.   Books with DRA codes 1. *Agawam Public Library*

Figure 2.2.   Books with DRA codes 2. *Agawam Public Library*

LIBRARY FUNDING

Funding is the means by which libraries pay the bills. Public schools and most public libraries are financially supported by local taxes—their local town or county municipalities. What they receive impacts what services they can offer, and can affect the quality of their services. The funding they receive may come from their state library through various programs, but these are in turn dependent on how well the state is funded by its governing body. In a 2015 *Library Journal* survey of U.S public libraries, it was found that 73 percent of the 416 that participated reported that their annual budgets increased by an average 4.3 percent over the preceding three years.[13] While this may be good news for them, not all public and school libraries do as well. There is a disturbing trend that often finds that when budgets get tight, the library is often the first to take the cut. Obviously less money equals fewer resources. Many libraries have not recovered from the financial crisis of 2008, and still more are treading water to stay solvent.

Some libraries are run, and funded, by an endowment, foundation, or other private sources. They are not a town department but are governed by an independent board of directors chosen or elected by the board itself. They are still public libraries if they meet requirements of a public library (as defined by their state library), but their funding is not managed or controlled by a municipality. Municipal library boards are usually appointed by the town clerk or other official.

Public libraries can also rely on other funding sources, such as grants from their state, their town, or from granting institutions. In Connecticut, principal public libraries (those which are the main or only library in a town) get an annual allotment from the state based on a formula. They may also get reimbursement funds for the interlibrary loan program—for the time and expense of providing and processing ILL to libraries in other towns. LSTA grants (Library Service and Technology Act) are administered by the U.S. Institute for Museum and Library Services (IMLS) and are the only federal program exclusively for libraries.

Community foundations can be found throughout the United States. (A community foundation is a grant making public charity created by and for a community of people.[14]) Typically they grant requests to nonprofits for programs, initiatives, materials, and equipment. Local Rotary Clubs, Lions Clubs, corporations, banks, businesses, and foundations also have grant programs to which libraries can apply for a specific program or materials. Grant writing is a time-consuming effort that may or may not pay off, as grantors only have so much money to give away. Virtually no grantors will give money for the general operating budget. Still, most public libraries do engage in grant writing as an integral part of their funding plan.

Libraries also participate in active fund-raising in the form of special activities such as dinners, concerts, or speakers, and through having an annual appeal or fund-raising campaign (usually conducted by mail or online). The budgets of some libraries are dependent on these successful events to supplement their funding or to provide a percentage of their annual budget.

Public libraries also rely on the help of "Friends of the Libraries" groups, whose mission it is to support and supplement the library's activities. Their fund-raisers—from book sales to plant sales to sponsored trips—help with materials or operations not funded by the library's regular budget. In some small public libraries, the Friends may be the sole source of funds for programming, entertainment media, and other items.

Most public school media centers rely on their town and come under the Board of Education budget. Money allocated for media centers may go directly to that library, or it may go through a central office that either doles it out to the individual libraries in the school system, does the purchasing for all the media centers in the system, or a combination of both. In these cases, the collection development for media centers may in fact be centralized—that is, someone in the central office, such as the director of media services, does all the selection and purchasing for all of the media centers in a school district. The media specialists may have their own lists of desired materials that are submitted to this central office buyer for consideration. In some cases, though, a media specialist is given a sum of money to do her own selecting. In the case of a middle school in Windsor, Connecticut, the librarian was allotted a budget of $25,400 in FY 2015/2016 for noninstructional supplies, books, subscriptions, instructional equipment repair, and new instructional equipment.[15]

Academic libraries are generally also funded by their parent institutions. State and local tax revenue is a major source of funding for public colleges and universities. Unlike private institutions, which may rely upon gifts and large endowments to help fund instruction, public two- and four-year colleges typically rely heavily on state and local appropriations.[16] Other possible monetary sources for all libraries include research grants, special projects, gifts and endowments, and fees for service.

It is worth noting that all of the above is dependent on the financial health of the granting body, and there is a trickle-down effect beginning at the federal level. "The Library Services and Technology Act (LSTA) is part of the annual Labor, Health and Human Services, and Education Appropriations bill. Also, the Innovative Approaches to Literacy (IAL) grant program from the U.S. Department of Education supports school libraries and nonprofit literacy organizations working to improve reading skills at the most critical early years of a child's development. While the majority of funding for libraries comes from state and local sources, federal funding provides critical assistance, giving libraries across the country the financial support they need to serve their communities."[17]

Likewise, if a town, city, or county is struggling to fund its community, the school and public libraries' budgets will be similarly impacted. Libraries usually have unqualified support of a community in principle, but the funding may not follow. It is often necessary for a town to take proactive measures to support library funding. An organization called EveryLibrary, a national nonprofit Public Action Committee (PAC) has as its mission to "help public, school, and college libraries win bonding, tax, and advisory referend[a], ensuring stable funding and access to libraries for generations to come. . . . [It] is a coalition partner with other organizations, associations, and non-profits that seek to support libraries through public awareness and advocacy."[18] Its board members and advisors are librarians and other advocates from all over the country. What this organization does as an organized campaign is what many communities must do on their own—that is, they must advocate to keep library funding intact.

What libraries need funding for, of course, is the staff, collection, technology, and myriad other expenses that go into running a library. Therefore, the library must have an idea of what funding it needs. They determine that by creating a budget.

Budgets

The Online Dictionary for Library and Information Science (ODLIS) defines a budget as "the total amount of funds available to meet a library's expenditures over a fixed period of time (usually one or two years). In most budgets, funds are allocated by category of expenditure, called lines."[19]

Library budgets follow the fiscal year (FY) of the funding organization—that is, the twelve-month period that an organization uses for budgeting. It is often from July 1 to June 30, particularly for school, academic, and most public libraries. A fiscal year can also follow a calendar year, running from January 1 to December 31, or the federal fiscal year, which runs from October 1 through September 30. It is identified by the month in which it ends, so FY 2017 would begin on October 1, 2016, and end on September 30, 2017. In some libraries, a change from the federal year to the school year is necessary to align with state and municipal grants and reports. For example, funding from a town may come in July, and all state reports are dated from July as well, but the library's fiscal year may begin in October. A challenge to keep track of, the problem was solved by the library's eventual migration to a July/June FY.

To develop a library budget, it is necessary to first determine what the library expects to accomplish. Having a long-range plan or a strategic plan can help, as it should already document the library's needs and what resources will be necessary to accomplish them. For example, if a library's plan is to replace twenty-five computers within five years at a rate of five per year, then the budget would spread that expense out over the five years. Changing priorities such as increased costs, new services, or staffing changes may require that some expenses be shifted within a budget, or even eliminated.

Before a budget can be created it is helpful if the person responsible for creating it knows the amount of funding available for the coming year, and the source of those funds. Depending on how a library is funded, it may be able to anticipate expected income based on recent budgets, although a percentage change up or down is not uncommon. In a neighboring town the public library was asked to make mid-year cuts due to a decrease in expected funding. It was also told that their next year's budget must come in another 5 percent lower. This is always problematic, and in what amounts to almost a Faustian bargain, the library must decide whether to cut staff, materials, or services in order to continue operation for the good of the community.

Programs and services will vary from library to library but the basics of budgeting will remain the same. The two main expenses will be personnel (wages and benefits) and collections; the remainder will be a smaller expense.[20] A typical, but by no means comprehensive, library operating expense budget request for any type of library may include line items or areas of funding such as:

TEXTBOX 2.2 SAMPLE BASIC OPERATING BUDGET

- Personnel
  - Salaries and wages
  - Benefits
- Collections
  - Printed books
  - Electronic books
  - Serials
  - Media
  - Database licensing
- Other operating expenses
  - Computers and other electronic equipment
  - Telecommunications
  - Utilities
  - Supplies
  - Insurance
  - Audit
  - Maintenance

These items may be broken down further. The Personnel line item can include lines for full-time, part-time, overtime, or unemployment compensation. In a large library, personnel may then be divided by position: director, librarian II, librarian I, library assistant, administrative, and so on. It may include separate lines for health insurance, retirement, and worker's compensation as well. Personnel costs are typically 60–80 percent of library expenditures.

Printed materials can be divided into such categories as fiction, nonfiction, juvenile, young adult; they can be even further divided by genres into adult fiction mysteries, romance, science fiction, and so on. Electronic materials would also be further broken down into additional budget items, or lines. Collections take up approximately 20 percent of expenditures.

Finally, a budget will have an area for other operating expenditures such as utilities, maintenance, audit, professional development, postage, insurance, heating cost, and programming; these expenses account for the balance of the budget—the remaining 10 percent or so. These three areas—personnel, collections, and other operating expenses—make up the basis for the expenses of a typical library budget.

The process would be for the library director to formulate a budget with input from department heads or other key personnel. Staying within the constraints of anticipated income, the proposed budget may then go to the library board for review. If the library is part of a school system, town, or college, it would be one segment of the entire budget. For example a school library is only one part of the Board of Education, and its budget would have to fit into a multipart budget. A town or county library is only one of many departments. The same goes for academic library budgets. All of these components go into the creation of a complete budget. Ideally the library's portion of the budget will be approved, but if the entire bottom line is too high, the library, and other departments, may be asked to make some cuts.

Ultimately the librarian must go through several steps in a budgetary process that involves presenting the proposed budget to the governing authority. It is a good idea to create a timeline since there may be multiple deadlines to be met. During my days as the director of a public library, this was one of the most stressful times of the year. The fiscal year began July 1 but a proposed budget would be due to the town by late January. It would be included in the multipage draft town budget (along with the other departments). This town has a style of government that includes several levels of oversight, requiring both public and committee meetings over the course of five months. A total of forty to fifty people are a part of this decision-making process, and it can be a grueling ordeal. It seems that the more people involved, the greater the chance for mistakes. In one memorable year, a representative at the final budget meeting proposed a new, lower, budget figure from the floor. As if that were not bad enough, it was seconded and passed without discussion. The library took quite a hit that year, and all of the hard work and good will that went on during the previous five months was out the window because of what amounted to one person's error—he was looking at a previous year's figures.

Some municipalities take the library budget to a referendum, which allows every registered voter to cast a ballot. This type of process gives all residents a say, which can work for or against the library depending on the current economic climate and the esteem in which the library is held. Organizations like the previously mentioned EveryLibrary, as well as local grassroots groups, are often pressed into service to support the library's funding during election time.

Considering how many people may have the authority to weigh in on it, there are four practical characteristics that your budget document should include:

1. *Clarity:* The budget presentation should be clear enough so every board member, every employee, and every municipal governing body member can understand what is being represented.
2. *Accuracy:* Budget documentation must support the validity of budget figures, and figures must be transcribed and reported carefully, without variation from the documentation.
3. *Consistency:* Budget presentations should retain the same format from period to period so that comparisons can be easily made. All budgets are comparative devices, used to show how what is being done now compares with what happened in the past and what is projected to happen in the future.
4. *Comprehensiveness:* Budget reports should include as complete a picture of fiscal activities as is possible. The only way to know the true cost of the library operation is to be certain that all revenue and expenditure categories are included within the budget.[21]

The modest sample budget that follows shows income versus expenditures as well as the amount budgeted. You'll notice that some numbers will stay the same from year to year and some will vary up or down. This will depend on a number of factors. When budgets are tight—and they almost always are—there may be little flexibility. The need for staff salary increases may result in a book or database budget remaining the same as the previous year. Decisions have to be made where cuts can be made, taking into account costs that cannot be altered, like utilities. Contracts may not be negotiable, but new vendors or contractors may be chosen if their prices rise too much. The goal is for expenses not to exceed income; in a best-case scenario income will exceed expenses and allow for carryover to the next year's budget.

Another element of the budget to consider is capital expenses. While the budgets we have been considering cover *operating* activities—those that recur regularly and can be anticipated from year to year—*capital* expenses are those that occur outside of the regular budget such as equipment replacement or new shelving, among others. These may require special fund-raising (such as a capital campaign) to accomplish.

CHAPTER SUMMARY

This chapter introduces the basic principles of collection development, management, and policies regarding library collections. This is accomplished by examining the elements of a collection policy and how they may differ by type of library. Particularly in school libraries and public library children's collections, the LSS should understand what must be taken into consideration to meet state and national standards when selecting materials for students at various reading levels. They must also understand where library funding comes from as well as the basics of how the budget process works.

Table 2.2. Sample Library Budget

Operating Income	2016 Actual	2017 Budget	2017 year end estimate	2018 Budget Request
Municipality	179,940	$185,338	$185,338	$190,898
County	$20,000	$20,600	$20,600	$20,600
State / library system	$375	$400	$400	$425
Federal (LSTA)	$0	$800	$800	$0
Funds carried forward	$4,500	$4,635	$4,635	$4,500
Fines, donations, fees	$3,800	$3,875	$3,875	$3,800
Operating Income Total	**$208,615**	**$215,648**	**$215,648**	**$220,223**

Operating Expenditures	2016 Actual	2017 Budget	2017 year end estimate	2018 Budget Request
Personnel				
Salaries and wages	$122,643	$ 126,322	$ 126,322	$130,116
Employee benefits	$12,850	$ 13,235	$ 13,235	$13,632
Personnel Subtotal	*$135,493*	*$139,557*	*$139,557*	*$143,748*
Collections				
Books	$17,600	$18,000	$18,000	$18,200
Periodicals	$3,400	$3,900	$3,900	$4,000
Video materials	$4,880	$5,380	$5,380	$5,380
Audio materials	$5,245	$5,845	$5,845	$5,845
Software and databases	$6,250	$6,500	$6,500	$6,500
Collections Subtotal	*$37,375*	*$39,625*	*$39,625*	*$39,925*
Other				
Contracted services	$10,520	$10,520	$10,520	$10,410
Continuing education	$2,500	$2,500	$2,500	$2,500
Programming	$2,640	$2,640	$2,640	$2,640
Telecommunications	$2,300	$2,355	$2,355	$2,400
Utilities	$5,162	$5,326	$5,326	$5,400
Equipment repair	$7,000	$7,500	$7,500	$7,500
Supplies	$5,625	$5,625	$5,625	$5,700
Other Subtotal	*$35,747*	*$36,466*	*$36,466*	*$36,550*
Operating Expenditures Total	**$208,615**	**$215,648**	**$215,648**	**$220,223**

DISCUSSION QUESTIONS

1. What are some of the elements of a collection policy? Do you agree with the inclusion of the Library Bill of Rights and the Freedom to Read statements? Explain your answer.
2. What are the basic elements of Common Core standards?
3. What are Lexile and DRA tools, and why are they used?
4. Describe several characteristics of a budget.
5. Public libraries that are municipally funded will have their budgets outlined in a document that is usually placed in the library for public review (e.g.,

Anytown Budget FY 2017). Compare the last two years of a town's library budget and note the differences, if any, in spending areas. What do you think may account for them?

ACTIVITIES

1. Prepare a bibliography with brief notations of two articles that identify basic principles and trends in collections. Your notations should be both descriptive and evaluative. Write a one-page essay about your findings.
2. Visit three libraries of varying type and size and ask for a copy of their collection policies. After reviewing the CDPs, are you able to see the collection principles reflected in the policies within the physical collections in the library? Which ones do you think are best?

NOTES

1. G. Edward Evans, Sheila S. Intner, and Jean Weihs, *Introduction to Technical Services*, 8th ed., Library and Information Science Text Series (Santa Barbara, CA: Libraries Unlimited, 2011), 60.

2. "Evaluating Your Collection: Best Practices for North Texas Libraries," North Texas Regional Library System, accessed April 8, 2016, http://ntrls.org/ConsultantReports/NTRLS_ EvaluatingYourCollection.pdf.

3. G. Edward Evans, Sheila S. Intner, and Jean Weihs, *Introduction to Technical Services*, 8th ed., Library and Information Science Text Series (Santa Barbara, CA: Libraries Unlimited, 2011), 82.

4. "Collection Development Policy," ALA.org, accessed December 2, 2015, http://ala.org.

5. Ibid.

6. "Library Bill of Rights," American Library Association, accessed December 3, 2015, http://www.ala.org/advocacy/intfreedom/librarybill.

7. "The Freedom to Read Statement," American Library Association, last modified June 30, 2004, accessed December 3, 2015, http://www.ala.org/advocacy/intfreedom/statementspols/freedomreadstatement.

8. "Workbook for Selection Policy Writing," American Library Association, last modified October 1999, accessed December 5, 2015, http://www.ala.org/bbooks/challengedmaterials/ preparation/workbook-selection-policy-writing.

9. "About the Standards," Common Core State Standards Initiative: Preparing America's Students for College and Career, accessed December 5, 2015, http://www.corestandards.org/ about-the-standards/.

10. Christopher Harris, "How to Get Started," *School Library Journal*, April 2012, 28.

11. Judith Rosen, "Publishers Respond to Common Core," *Publishers Weekly*, last modified October 28, 2013, accessed December 9, 2015, http://www.publishersweekly.com/pw/ by-topic/industry-news/publisher-news/article/59720-publishers-respond-to-common-core. html.

12. "Learn about Leveled Reading," Scholastic, accessed December 7, 2015, http://www. scholastic.com/parents/resources/article/book-selection-tips/learn-about-leveled-reading.

13. Lisa Peet, "Paying for People," *Library Journal* 140, no. 2 (February 1, 2015): 30.

14. "About Community Foundations," The Community Foundations National Standards Board, accessed December 7, 2015, http://www.cfstandards.org/about-community-foundations.

15. Rachel Bray, e-mail interview by the author, Sage Park Middle School, Windsor, CT, December 18, 2015.

16. Michael Mitchell and Michael Leachman, "Years of Cuts Threaten to Put College Out of Reach for More Students," Center on Budget and Policy Priorities, last modified May 13, 2015, accessed December 7, 2015, http://www.cbpp.org/research/state-budget-and-tax/years-of-cuts-threaten-to-put-college-out-of-reach-for-more-students.

17. "Appropriations," American Library Association Government Relations, accessed December 9, 2015, http://www.ala.org/advocacy/advleg/federallegislation/libraryfunding.

18. "About Us," EveryLibrary, accessed December 9, 2015, http://everylibrary.org/about-everylibrary/.

19. Joan M. Reitz, "ODLIS Online Dictionary for Library and Information Science," ODLIS, last modified January 10, 2013, accessed December 10, 2015, http://www.abc-clio.com/ODLIS/odlis_about.aspx.

20. Christine Lind Hage, *The Public Library Start-up Guide* (Chicago, IL: American Library Association, 2004), 48.

21. "AE 13: Developing the Library Budget," Public Library Development, accessed December 10, 2015, http://pld.dpi.wi.gov/pld_ae13.

REFERENCES, SUGGESTED READINGS, AND WEBSITES

American Library Association. "Collection Development Policy." ala.org. Accessed December 2, 2015. http://ala.org.

———. "Appropriations." American Library Association Government Relations. Accessed December 9, 2015. http://www.ala.org/advocacy/advleg/federallegislation/libraryfunding.

———. "Diversity in Collection Development: An Interpretation of the Library Bill of Rights." ala.org. Accessed December 2, 2015. http://www.ala.org/advocacy/intfreedom/librarybill/interpretations/diversitycollection.

———. "The Freedom to Read Statement." American Library Association. Last modified June 30, 2004. Accessed December 3, 2015. http://www.ala.org/advocacy/intfreedom/statementspols/freedomreadstatement.

———. "Library Bill of Rights." American Library Association. Accessed December 3, 2015. http://www.ala.org/advocacy/intfreedom/librarybill.

———. "Library Operating Expenditures: A Selected Annotated Bibliography ALA Library Fact Sheet 4." American Library Association. Last modified April 2015. Accessed December 13, 2015. http://www.ala.org/tools/libfactsheets/alalibraryfactsheet04.

———. "Workbook for Selection Policy Writing." American Library Association. Last modified October 1999. Accessed December 5, 2015. http://www.ala.org/bbooks/challengedmaterials/preparation/workbook-selection-policy-writing.

Bray, Rachel. E-mail interview by the author. Sage Park Middle School, Windsor, CT. December 18, 2015.

Common Core State Standards Initiative. "About the Standards." Common Core State Standards Initiative: Preparing America's Students for College and Career. Accessed December 5, 2015. http://www.corestandards.org/about-the-standards/.

Council of Foundations. "About Community Foundations." The Community Foundations National Standards Board. Accessed December 7, 2015. http://www.cfstandards.org/about-community-foundations.

Edwards, Julie Biondo. "Community Centered: 23 Reasons Why Your Library Is the Most Important Place in Town." Public Libraries Online. Last modified April 30, 2013. Accessed December 3, 2015. http://publiclibrariesonline.org/2013/04/community-centered-23-reasons-why-your-library-is-the-most-important-place-in-town/.

Evans, G. Edward, Sheila S. Intner, and Jean Weihs. *Introduction to Technical Services*. 8th ed. Library and Information Science Text Series. Santa Barbara, CA: Libraries Unlimited, 2011.

EveryLibrary. "About Us." EveryLibrary. Accessed December 9, 2015. http://everylibrary.org/about-everylibrary/.

Groton Public Library Board. "Policy Manual of the Groton Public Library." Groton Public Library. Last modified July 15, 2015. Accessed December 5, 2015. http://www.groton-ct.gov/library/docs/Library%20Policy%20Manual.pdf.

Hage, Christine Lind. *The Public Library Start-up Guide*. Chicago, IL: American Library Association, 2004.

Harris, Christopher. "How to Get Started." *School Library Journal*, April 2012, 28.

Mitchell, Michael, and Michael Leachman. "Years of Cuts Threaten to Put College Out of Reach for More Students." Center on Budget and Policy Priorities. Last modified May 13, 2015. Accessed December 7, 2015. http://www.cbpp.org/research/state-budget-and-tax/years-of-cuts-threaten-to-put-college-out-of-reach-for-more-students.

North Texas Regional Library System. "Evaluating Your Collection: Best Practices for North Texas Libraries." North Texas Regional Library System. Accessed April 8, 2016. http://ntrls.org/ConsultantReports/NTRLS_EvaluatingYourCollection.pdf.

Peet, Lisa. "Paying for People." *Library Journal* 140, no. 2 (February 1, 2015): 30.

Reitz, Joan M. "ODLIS Online Dictionary for Library and Information Science." ODLIS. Last modified January 10, 2013. Accessed December 10, 2015. http://www.abc-clio.com/ODLIS/odlis_about.aspx.

Rosen, Judith. "Publishers Respond to Common Core." *Publishers Weekly*. Last modified October 28, 2013. Accessed December 9, 2015. http://www.publishersweekly.com/pw/by-topic/industry-news/publisher-news/article/59720-publishers-respond-to-common-core.html.

Scholastic, Inc. "Learn About Leveled Reading." Scholastic. Accessed December 7, 2015. http://www.scholastic.com/parents/resources/article/book-selection-tips/learn-about-leveled-reading.

Smith, G. Stevenson. *Managerial Accounting for Libraries and Other Not-for-profit Organizations*. 2nd ed. Chicago, IL: ALA, 2002.

Wisconsin Department of Public Instruction. "AE 13: Developing the Library Budget." Public Library Development. Accessed December 10, 2015. http://pld.dpi.wi.gov/pld_ae13.

CHAPTER 3

Selection

LSS assist with decisions regarding selection, deselection, retention, and replacement of all types of library resources, and can use the recognized standard evaluative sources to assist with collection development. (ALA-LSSC Competencies #3 and #7)

Topics Covered in This Chapter:
- Selection Philosophies
- Selection Criteria
- Evaluative Sources
  - Print
  - Nonprint
  - Serials
- Verification of Materials

Key Terms:

Freedom to Read Statement: The Freedom to Read Statement is a document created by the American Library Association (ALA, the national professional library association) to affirm that libraries make available the widest diversity of views and expressions.[1]

ISBN: The ISBN is the International Standard Book Number, a unique thirteen-digit number assigned to each edition of a work. The same title published in regular text, large print, or on CD will each have a different ISBN. It is the most reliable method of verification. The ISBN is divided into elements representing prefix, country, publisher, format, and check digit. The check digit is a number that is used for error protection.[2]

Library Bill of Rights: The Library Bill of Rights is a document created by the American Library Association (ALA, the national professional library association), affirming basic policies that guide library service. It is based on the principles of the U.S. Constitution and guides librarians in providing equal service to all patrons.[3]

Nonprint materials: Nonprint, or nonbook items, are those that are not paper based and include electronic books, full-text serial databases, electronic newspapers, and media such as CDs, DVDs, Blu-Ray, and Playaways. These materials represent a large part of a library's collection, and their selection is evaluated in several different ways.

Selection: The selection of materials for inclusion in a library follows a set of criteria, often found in a library collection development policy. Criteria include, but are not limited to, the reputation of the author, authoritativeness, literary style, timeliness of subject, readability, and format.

Serials: "Serials" is an all-inclusive term covering a variety of publications in various forms, content, and purpose, like magazines and newspapers. They are issued in successive parts, at regular intervals, and are intended to continue indefinitely.[4]

Verification: This means that the bibliographic information of an item must be confirmed for accuracy. This is done for several reasons: to be sure that the item actually exists, and to determine if it is needed for the collection. It is also needed to determine if the bibliographic data provided is correct. This insures that the correct item in the correct format is chosen for the collection.

SELECTION PHILOSOPHIES

Tax supported public libraries are a relatively modern concept, beginning in the United States in the mid- to late 1800s; Boston Public Library is one of the most recognizable. By the end of that century the concept flourished and many cities and towns had them. Not all public libraries are funded by their town or municipality; many, particularly in New England, were privately endowed and given to their town as a gift by philanthropists and are run by a board of directors. Originally education was the primary emphasis of a public library.

The rise of the novel, and recreational reading in general, was viewed with a jaundiced eye as the prevailing morals required that novels reflect the community standards of the time. A librarian selecting books then was encouraged to choose those of good moral and instructional value. Libraries today must select from a much wider variety of possible publications and media—and for a vastly diverse population.

One philosophy was to give patrons what they need, not what they want. At a library board meeting in the very early 1980s at a small endowed New England library, an elderly board member who subscribed to that philosophy asked the librarian for a copy of *Aesop's Fables*. Then he took out his pocket watch to time her to see how long it took to find it! His point was that classics should be readily available to anyone at any time. Today, however, many librarians subscribe to the "just in time, not just in case" theory of selection. The belief is that libraries should be selecting what the public wants *now*, not underused volumes that take up much needed space. With the range of options available to libraries such as interlibrary loan, digital books, and electronic delivery, a library doesn't need to own every title that a patron may request, but can still provide it using alternative resources.

Most libraries today also endorse the principles in the Library Bill of Rights and the Freedom to Read Statement as part of their philosophies, committing to upholding the rights of individuals to access whatever material they choose. Even if that information is controversial or unacceptable to others, libraries must make sure that they provide a balanced collection representing a diversity of viewpoints. This also means that individual selectors cannot impose their biases or weaknesses into the process. A selection philosophy of free and open access to all is at the core of libraries today.

A corollary to the selection philosophy is the process of evaluating the collection for retention and deselection as well. No library can continually collect without carefully and systematically inventorying items for retention or deselection for reasons including the age and condition of the materials, their relevance, and their current appeal. Out-of-date items not only take up precious space but can also provide a disservice to a library if the item is in poor condition, the material is not current, or is just plain wrong. Old, however, does not necessarily connote obsolescence. This concept will be discussed further in chapter 6.

SELECTION CRITERIA

There are a number of things to consider when selecting materials, such as the subject matter, the author's reputation, the demand (which takes the library's demographics into account), cost, and format. As difficult as it may be, the selector must also turn off his or her preferences or biases and choose materials that represent all points of view. With all that to consider, and so much out there to choose from, this can be a daunting task.

Often included as part of a collection policy, the following list represents some of the standard criteria one may consider:

TEXTBOX 3.1 SELECTION CRITERIA[5]

a. Reputation or significance of an author or artist
b. Authoritativeness and accuracy
c. Literary style or artistic excellence
d. Relevance to present or anticipated needs and interests of the community in terms of new materials as well as duplication of materials in high demand
e. Permanent value as resource material
f. Timeliness, reflecting new areas of knowledge or changing conditions of the contemporary scene
g. Relation to existing materials in the library's collection
h. Readability and clarity in relation to the intended audience
i. Availability within other collections in our cooperative database
j. Suitability of format for library use
k. Price and availability of funds
l. Local interest

Schools and academic libraries will follow the same selection rules but would have additional criteria relevant to their institutions.

**TEXTBOX 3.2 ADDITIONAL CRITERIA
FOR SCHOOL AND ACADEMIC LIBRARIES**

1. Requests of faculty and students
2. Overall purpose and educational significance of materials
3. Validity, timeliness or permanence, and appropriateness of material
4. Contribution the subject matter makes to the curriculum and the interests of the students
5. Materials support and are consistent with the educational philosophy, goals, and objectives of the school district.
6. Materials are appropriate for the age, emotional development, reading ability, cognitive level, learning styles, and social development of the students with whom they will be used.
7. Materials are used in active, productive ways that foster teaching and learning.
8. Materials depict the cultural diversity of our world.

As noted in textbox 3.1, format is a major concern. Most books commercially available today have what is called a perfect binding: glue is applied to the spine of gathered pages of a book and then glued again into the cover. Books bound this way are quite durable but do not have a very long shelf life, so to speak, and can fall apart or lose pages as they age and the glue dries out. Books that are "library bound" are sewn first, then glued into the cover. This is much sturdier and allows for much longer use, but this kind of binding is usually only available for children's titles, is more expensive, and may outlast the usefulness of the materials.

Some books are spiral bound, also known as a comb binding. This method uses a metal or plastic coil to create a binding that is flexible, easy to open, and can come in a variety of colors. While popular for some materials, a spiral binding is not usually a first choice for libraries as the pages are more easily torn out and the spine itself is usually too narrow for placing a call number.

Another format concern when selecting books is size. Those that are very small or oversized can potentially pose problems for shelving. Media is also a consideration, as CDs, DVDs, Playaways (an all-in-one audiobook format with a preloaded title), and microforms (micro-reproductions of documents on film) can require special shelving.

Factors used to determine the selection, retention, or cancellation, of periodicals include:

- Use (or circulation history)
- Importance of the title to the library
- Relevance of the content to the library's collection and to the school or college's curriculum
- Cost

Books and printed material are still the largest percentage of materials purchased by libraries but nonbook items such as electronic books, print and full-text serial databases, print and electronic newspapers, and media represent a large part of a library's collection. "While traditional collection development criteria, such as subject, level, and target audience apply to the selection of most e-resources, the management of the electronic format is more complex and, as such, it is good practice to develop a supplementary policy which addresses specific format related issues. Such a policy should be used in conjunction with the more traditional collection development policy and not in isolation."[6] Elements would include:

TEXTBOX 3.3 ADDITIONAL CRITERIA FOR ELECTRONIC SELECTION

Technical feasibility such as

- availability and compatibility of the e-resources with existing hardware
- functionality and reliability including search and retrieval, and reliability of the source
- vendor support
- licensing issues

Other considerations are currency and accuracy of information, as some electronic resources lag behind the print version.

Also, the electronic resource should provide sufficient added value over the print equivalent.[7]

EVALUATIVE SOURCES

Print

There is a lot of paper-based material available to the library such as books, serials, and newspapers. Fortunately there are a number of sources available to help determine what to select. First among them are the professional review journals which offer critical and unbiased reviews.

Publishers put out catalogs of their offerings, which provide cover art and descriptions of their materials. Unlike an objective review these descriptions are always positive. Catalogs can be a useful resource as it allows the selector to see what the books look like, see sample pages, and what books may be included in a series. They are no substitute for a qualified review, but they do provide for a visual display and a description. Baker and Taylor offers selection help such as their Opening Day Collections and Selection List services.

Speaking of reviews, bad reviews don't mean there will be no demand for a particular title. Patrons want to read what they want to read, regardless. At one time a popular comedian wrote an autobiography; the reviews were not kind. After a

TEXTBOX 3.4 REVIEW JOURNALS

For all libraries the most authoritative journals that review books and serials include:

- *Library Journal*
- *Booklist*
- *Publishers Weekly*
- *Book Page*
- *New York Times Book Review*
- *Kirkus Reviews*

Additionally for school media centers and children's literature there are:

- *School Library Journal*
- *Horn Book*
- *Bulletin of the Center for Children's Books*

For academic libraries:

- *Choice* is the most widely used journal.

There are also numerous journals for subject specialties such as computers and information technology, law, and other subjects.

number of requests from patrons the book was added to the collection in my library. Everyone who checked it out brought it back quickly, usually with the added comment that it wasn't very good. On the other hand, there are books that get the most favorable of reviews, but turn out to be unreadable.

Other standard resources for selection include bibliographies such as the H. W. Wilson series, which include Fiction Core Collection and Public Library Core Collection: Non-Fiction for Public Libraries; Children's, Middle and Junior High Core Collections; as well as Senior High Core Collections; Graphic Novels Core Collections; and for academic as well as public libraries, core collections in subject areas such as history, biography, and science.

There are also a number of online booklists such as the websites NoveList, What Should I Read Next, Epic Reads, Goodreads, and so on—all of which can give selectors suggested titles with plot summaries and, in some cases, cited reviews. Libraries and bookstores are also a source for bibliographies of local reading groups and book clubs. In selecting materials don't discount the professional knowledge and judgment of staff and colleagues.

Library patrons have always suggested titles, and popular media such as magazines, talk shows, and newspapers, while not necessarily critical review sources, are frequently where patrons will first hear of something new they'd like to read. Oprah has become a phenomenon in that realm. Patron suggestions have been taken a step further with the relatively new, more formal process, called Demand Driven Acqui-

Figure 3.1. Evaluative sources. *Bill Memorial Library*

sition (DDA) or Patron Driven Acquisition (PDA); this will be discussed in the next chapter when we look more closely at the acquisition process.

Nonprint

Nonprint materials encompass a wide range of resources: electronic books, electronic serials, audiovisual materials such as CDs, DVDs and Blu-Ray, and databases.

Many of them can be evaluated through the same sources previously cited, as professional journals routinely review media, and the electronic version of a book is often included in the print review.

Nonprint also includes media, and any list of all available media is bound to be out-of-date by the time it is published. New technologies and new combinations of older forms seem to appear daily. Just when one thinks that the latest developments have been identified and a decision to invest money in the equipment and software has been made, a new, even more exciting and potentially valuable format appears. With these limitations in mind, the following is offered as an extensive but not exhaustive list of media useful in the library:

TEXTBOX 3.5 SAMPLE MEDIA FOUND IN A LIBRARY

- Audiotapes
- Films
- Filmstrips (with and w/out sound)
- Flat pictures (photos, illustrations, posters, artwork)
- Games (usually educational)
- Globes
- Laser formats (including holograms)
- Maps (flat and relief)
- Microforms (all types)
- Mixed media packages (kits)
- Opaque projector materials
- Phonograph records
- Printed music
- Realia (toys)
- Slides
- Specimen collections
- Video formats
- Working models
- Software
- DVDs
- CDs
- TV (closed circuit or satellite)
- LCD projectors
- Digital cameras
- Video cameras

In the case of current or classic movies on CD or Blu-Ray, reviews are readily available in newspapers, popular magazines, and on television, radio, and the Internet. Once again, a good or bad review can be less important than patron demand. All of the above can be accessed through various commercial sources such as Baker and Taylor's Scene and Heard AV service for music, CD, and video titles. Ingram, another source of books and media, offers what they term "curation services" to aid in selection.

Figure 3.2. Sample media found in a library. *Bill Memorial Library*

Serials

"Serials," (also known as periodicals) is an all-inclusive term covering a variety of publications of various forms, content, and purpose, like magazines and news-papers. They are issued in successive parts, at regular intervals, and are intended to continue indefinitely.

Ulrich's Periodicals Directory, a global source for periodicals information since 1932, is the "authoritative source of bibliographic and publisher information" on more than 300,000 periodicals of all types of "academic and scholarly journals, Open Access publications, peer-reviewed titles, popular magazines, newspapers, newsletters and more from around the world."[8] In print since 1932 it is also avail-able on the Web. *Ulrich's* is international in scope, provides unbiased collection of data, and is updated daily. They are not the only source, as vendors such as EBSCO or WT.Cox provide a comprehensive catalog of available titles, prices, availability, and other details, as well.

VERIFICATION OF MATERIALS

Once titles are identified they have to be bibliographically verified—that is, the information must be confirmed for accuracy. This is done for several reasons: to be sure that the item actually exists, and to determine if it is needed for the collection. It is also needed to determine if the bibliographic data provided is correct.

If the item is located in a review journal or other print or nonprint source, the understanding is that the citation is correct—although it isn't always. Occasionally an ISBN will be incorrect, as well as the spelling of the author's name, title, and so on. In some cases a title may have been changed during the publication process, but the resource hasn't caught up to it. The chance of mistaken information increases in the case of a request from a user, staff member, or faculty. Fortunately there is a process to follow:

1. The request is received.
2. Requests are sorted, particularly if requests come from several sources in the library.
3. The request is then verified for accuracy of author, title, edition, publication date, ISBN, and format. This can be done by checking reliable sources:
   a. The library's OPAC
   b. The local consortium
   c. Library of Congress
   d. WorldCat
   e. OCLC
4. It is the job of the LSS performing this work to determine if the library needs the requested item, as it could be:
   a. A duplicate of an existing copy
   b. A replacement for a lost copy
   c. An extra copy due to demand
5. As most library databases can display a title even if it is not yet received, verify its status to determine if:
   a. It is on order
   b. It is in process
   c. It is part of a standing order

Then group the requests by type: print, nonprint, serial, or media. When doing so, include the source of the request so that anyone who looks at the record or the order can tell what department asked for it; the source of funds, or where in the budget it fits; and the source of supply, or how it will be obtained.

Other considerations in the verification process are to determine what format you are ordering. It is easy to confuse the ISBNs and order a regular print version of a title that was supposed to be ordered in large print, a CD instead of a book, a print book instead of the electronic version, or a DVD instead of a Blu-Ray. Carelessness in verification can be costly as materials ordered by "operator error" may not be returnable.

There are occasions when it is necessary to order older books. In that case it must be determined if the item is current or still in print. Even if a book is out of print there are ways of locating copies through out-of-print dealers, either private businesses or established concerns such as Abebooks, Alibris, Biblio, e-Bay, half.com, or even Amazon. This is not as easy for a nonprint item, but not impossible.

CHAPTER SUMMARY

In this chapter we were introduced to the philosophy of selection along with the criteria used to select materials in all formats such as the reputation of the author, the accuracy and timeliness of the subject, suitability, local interest, and the cost. Deselection and retention of materials was introduced, as well as the concept of bibliographic verification of selected materials to ensure the accuracy of the item and its need to be included in the collection.

DISCUSSION QUESTIONS

1. Explain what is meant by the "just in time" versus "just in case" philosophy of collection development; what problems does it solve?
2. For print books, many criteria were suggested for selection. Of those criteria, which three do you view as most important and why?
3. Review some materials catalogs and online book lists. How are they helpful, and what information do they provide?
4. Using a professional review journal, read three reviews of books or media on a similar topic and explain why you might choose one item over another. What in the review influenced your decision?
5. Explain how and why one would verify bibliographic information of selected materials.

ACTIVITIES

1. Select a book title from the *New York Times* Best Seller list (or other national best-seller list). Look at reviews of the book from several sources (published books review journals and magazines, websites, Amazon reviews, publisher sites, author sites, etc.). Which reviews did you find most helpful in deciding if this was a title you would like to select for your library? Which were not as helpful and why?

NOTES

1. "The Freedom to Read Statement," American Library Association, accessed December 17, 2015, http://www.ala.org/advocacy/intfreedom/statementspols/freedomreadstatement.
2. "What is an ISBN?," International ISBN Agency, last modified 2014, accessed December 23, 2015, https://www.isbn-international.org/content/what-isbn.
3. "Library Bill of Rights," American Library Association, accessed December 17, 2015, http://www.ala.org/advocacy/sites/ala.org.advocacy/files/content/intfreedom/librarybill/lbor.pdf.
4. "What is a serial?" Cataloger's Reference Shelf, accessed December 25, 2015, http://www.itsmarc.com/crs/mergedprojects/conser/conser/module_2_1__ccm.htm.
5. "Policy Manual of Groton Public Library," Groton Public Library, last modified July 15, 2015, accessed December 18, 2015, http://www.groton-ct.gov/library/docs/Library%20Policy%20Manual.pdf.

6. Johnson Sharon et al., "Key Issues for E-Resource Collection Development: A Guide for Libraries," The International Federation of Library Associations and Institutions, last modified August 2012, accessed December 18, 2015, http://www.ifla.org/publications/key-issues-for-e-resource-collection-development-a-guide-for-libraries.

7. Ibid.

8. "Frequently Asked Questions," Ulrichsweb, accessed December 20, 2015, http://www.ulrichsweb.com/ulrichsweb/faqs.asp.

REFERENCES, SUGGESTED READINGS, AND WEBSITES

American Library Association. "The Freedom to Read Statement." American Library Association. Accessed December 17, 2015. http://www.ala.org/advocacy/intfreedom/statementspols/freedomreadstatement.

———. "Library Bill of Rights." American Library Association. Accessed December 17, 2015. http://www.ala.org/advocacy/sites/ala.org.advocacy/files/content/intfreedom/librarybill/lbor.pdf.

Bangert, Stephanie Rogers. "Thinking Boldly! College and University Library Mission Statements as Roadsigns to the Future." Association of College and Research Libraries. Accessed December 18, 2015. http://www.ala.org/acrl/publications/whitepapers/nashville/bangert.

CONSER. "What Is a serial?" Cataloger's Reference Shelf. Accessed December 25, 2015. http://www.itsmarc.com/crs/mergedprojects/conser/conser/module_2_1__ccm.htm.

International ISBN Agency. "What Is an ISBN?" International ISBN Agency. Last modified 2014. Accessed December 23, 2015. https://www.isbn-international.org/content/what-isbn.

Proquest. "Frequently Asked Questions." Ulrichsweb. Accessed December 20, 2015. http://www.ulrichsweb.com/ulrichsweb/faqs.asp.

Sharon, Johnson, Ole Gunnar Evensen, Julia Gelfand, Glenda Lammera, Lynn Sipe, and Nadia Zilper. "Key Issues for E-Resource Collection Development: A Guide for Libraries." The International Federation of Library Associations and Institutions. Last modified August 2012. Accessed December 18, 2015. http://www.ifla.org/publications/key-issues-for-e-resource-collection-development-a-guide-for-libraries.

Shaw, Marie Keen. *Library Technology and Digital Resources: An Introduction for Support Staff.* Library Support Staff Handbooks. Lanham, MD: Rowman and Littlefield, 2015.

St. Edward's University. "Selection Criteria for Journal Subscriptions." St. Edward's University Munday Library. Last modified 2014. Accessed December 19, 2015. http://library.stedwards.edu/about/policies/collection-development.

Thornton-Verma, Henrietta. "Databases: What You're Loving, What's Upcoming." Last modified November 1, 2013. Accessed December 19, 2015. http://search.ebscohost.com/login.aspx?direct=true&db=aph&AN=83527001&authtype=cookie,cpid&custid=s1024272&site=ehost-live&scope=site.

Town of Groton, CT. "Policy Manual of Groton Public Library." Groton Public Library. Last modified July 15, 2015. Accessed December 18, 2015. http://www.groton-ct.gov/library/docs/Library%20Policy%20Manual.pdf.

CHAPTER 4

Acquisitions

LSS know the various ways in which content, in multiple formats, is produced and distributed to libraries. LSS know the basic principles and can apply the appropriate procedures to the processes that provide users access to a wide variety of content. (ALA-LSSC Competencies #4 and #5)

Topics Covered in This Chapter:
- The Publishing Industry
  - Mainstream Publishers
  - Independent and Small Press Publishers
  - Electronic Publishers
  - Government Information
- Vendors
- Acquisition Procedures
  - Print
  - Nonprint
  - Gifts and Exchange
  - Outsourcing
    - DDA/PDA/UDA
- Receiving

Key Terms:
Acquisitions: The acquisition of materials in a library means ordering and receiving print and nonprint materials. It does not refer to the selection of these materials, nor does it refer to the ordering of office supplies or library equipment. The former is done by collection development or selection staff; the latter by the business or technical services department.

DDA/PDA/UDA: Demand-driven acquisition and patron-driven acquisition, also known as use-driven acquisitions, is a method that allows patrons to contribute to the acquisition of materials for library collection through an electronic program in the user's catalog.

Government information: Government information may also be referred to as public information. It is defined as information created, compiled, and/or maintained by the federal government that is owned by the people and held in trust by the government and should be available to all.

Outsourcing: Outsourcing is another way that libraries can acquire materials by contracting with a service that does the selection and processing without input from the staff. This can take the entire acquisition function out of the library.

Publishers: A publisher taps the sources of material, usually through agents and editors. It raises and supplies the capital or funds to run the publishing operation, aids in the development of the material, provides for the legal work necessary, distributes and promotes the material, and maintains the records of the organization.

Vendors: Vendors, also known as jobbers or wholesalers, are a third party that buys print and nonprint materials from publishers to resell to public, school, and academic libraries at a discount. They provide the advantage of "one-stop shopping"—they can supply materials from a variety of publishers.

THE PUBLISHING INDUSTRY

The first thing to determine is what a publisher is and what it does.

Mainstream Publishers

A publisher performs several functions:

- Taps the sources of material, usually through agents and editors (unsolicited manuscripts are discouraged)
- Raises and supplies the capital, or funds, to run the publishing operation
- Aids in the development of the material by editing, for example
- Provides for the legal work necessary such as issuing contracts
- Distributes and promotes the material to the public
- Maintains the records of the organization in relation to sales, contracts, and so on

There are many different types of traditional print publishers. Those that we refer to as **mainstream**, or major commercial publishers, offer several kinds of publications including *trade books*, which are geared to a wide general audience accessed through bookstores and libraries. Examples include Simon and Schuster, Harper-Collins, Penguin Random House, and Houghton-Mifflin Harcourt. Trade books are usually offered in hardbound volumes.

Paperback books, on the other hand, are found in two categories. The first is called *quality trade paperback*, which includes high-demand paperbacks from widely distributed publishers. They are often titles reprinted after a successful hardback run. A trade paperback is larger than its mass market cousin and may even originate in this format. *Mass market paperbacks* are those standard rack-sized books found in retail outlets and airports. They can include popular authors and titles as well as genre fiction such as romance or mystery stories.

While commercial publishers focus on making money by publishing for the popular audience, *University presses* publish works of scholarly, intellectual, or creative merit, often for a small audience of specialists.[1] However, these nonfiction and academic materials can appeal to all libraries, depending on the subject, and to academic libraries in particular. This is not the same as *textbooks* that are generally technical, reference, or professional. They have limited sales volume.

Independent and Small Press Publishers

Often referred to as **small press**, **independent publishers** differ from commercial or mainstream publishers primarily by the size of their budget and output, with sales under a predetermined dollar amount, or by the limited number of books published or in print at a given point in time. There are many commercially viable independent and small presses, and authors often find that the service and attention of such a business can be more personal and hands-on. Contrary to what some think, a small press can produce books that are every bit as diverse as large commercial publishers. While they do not have the large costs and vast sales required, they can produce books for a smaller market at a reasonable cost and still make a profit. Small presses can also produce books more quickly than the big guys.[2] Some well-known independent and small press publishers that fall into this category include Beacon Press, Pegasus Books, Cleis Press, Down East Books, and Tantor Media.

Included under the small press umbrella are vanity presses, also known as vanity publishers or subsidized publishers. At one time this was the only way for an author to self-publish. There are no selection criteria, and an author would assume all costs to have their book published. The author is also responsible for any leftover stock. Using such a press may be an expensive option. Where a traditional publisher purchases the right to publish and sell a manuscript, a vanity press charges a fee to produce a book. This may be an appropriate choice for those wanting a small run of family genealogy, memoirs, or recipe collections. However, reviewers or bloggers may ignore such a title, and bookstores and libraries may not carry them.

The better option these days are reputable print-on-demand services offered online such as Amazon's Createspace, Lulu, or Blurb. These services offer design tools for editing, design, and marketing, and may offer some distribution services. Some also offer, for a price, professional editing packages. This market has become so large that *Publishers Weekly* offers a site called BookLife devoted to self-published materials. Through their PW Select service they offer tips and marketing advice, as well as the option to submit their books for PW review.[3]

Finally, there is a category of small presses that deal with special or rare materials. These companies, such as Higginson Books, produce original works and reprints of rare and out-of-print genealogies and local histories. Although located in Salem, Massachusetts, they offer coverage of such materials from all over the United States.[4]

Electronic Publishers

Electronic publishing has provided us with relatively easy access to textbooks, serials, e-books, and e-readers. It is expensive relative to paper books as access to electronic content may require subscriptions, fees, and special devices, and there may be some limited-use restrictions. However, it can provide a large amount of content to a large group of users at the same time.

E-books have become a regular part of library circulation, and libraries routinely subscribe to popular services such as Overdrive, a digital distributor of electronic books, music, and video, and Axis 360, a digital media service of Baker & Taylor (other providers include ProQuest E-book Central/MyiLibrary and Ingram Libraries); they then choose the titles they want to offer according to what they can afford to invest. These products allow library users to log in through their circulation system and choose titles to download to their devices for viewing or listening; they can even stream video. It requires that users have a compatible device like a Kindle, Nook, Kobo, or Sony e-reader, tablet, or smartphone. The library has some control over setting loan periods, but these titles cannot be renewed. When the due date arrives, the titles disappear from the device.

Libraries do not own the content that they download. It is proprietary to the owner of the service. Also, the cost per title is much higher than the same title sold commercially. For example, a current best seller may be available to purchase for one's own device for $15.99 on Amazon but may cost $85.00 to purchase in Overdrive (because it will serve multiple users for multiple circulations). If a library chooses to withdraw from one of these electronic providers, they lose all of the content they have paid for. Additionally, some e-books may be licensed for only a limited number of circulations. Because of the popularity and demand, there can be unreasonably long waiting periods for popular titles. Many patrons had complained that they had trouble downloading the software or logging on, or found that new titles have a long wait list. To my consternation, many patrons simply found it easier to purchase the title they want to read from a commercial source. Whatever method one chooses, there is no doubt that electronic publishing can bring immediate satisfaction.

Another way that libraries can provide electronic content is by purchasing compatible devices and loading them with electronic books through any number of sources, then loaning them out to patrons. All of the titles purchased for that device remain there.

There are, fortunately, free sources of electronically published materials, such as Project Gutenberg (a digital library of free public domain e-books), e-books on EB-SCOhost (formerly NetLibrary), Oxford Text Archive (over two thousand classical texts) and PlanetPDF e-books—a collection of classic novels in PDF format. Also to be considered is the Google Books Library Project, whose goal is "to work with publishers and libraries to create a comprehensive, searchable, virtual card catalog of all books in all languages that helps users discover new books and publishers discover new readers."[5] It has not been without controversy.

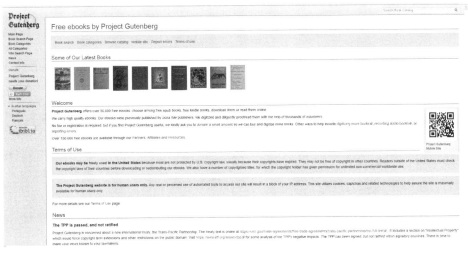

Figure 4.1.   Screenshot of Project Gutenberg. *Courtesy of the author*

Government Information

Government information may also be referred to as public information. It is defined as:

- Information *created, compiled*, and/or maintained by the federal government
- Information that is *owned* by the people
- Information that is *held in trust* by the government
- Information that should be *available to all*

It consists of information provided by all three branches of the federal government, and includes Congressional Records, Supreme Court reports, reports of individual departments, and information provided by all branches of state governments and agencies. Government information is kept in depository libraries, in what is known as the Federal Depository Library Program. Depository libraries are so designated by congressional appointment. However, much of government information is now available online through the Federal Digital System, or www.gpo.gov/fdsys/. The Government Printing Office, or GPO, is an amazing source of current, free, or inexpensive publications of government offices and divisions that can be a valuable addition to a library's collection. Acquisition is directly through the GPO at www.gpo.gov.

VENDORS

Vendors, also known as jobbers or wholesalers, are a form of outsourcing, as they are a third party that buys books from the publishers to resell to public, school, and academic libraries at a discount. They provide the advantage of "one-stop shopping"—they can supply materials from a variety of publishers.

Figure 4.2. Government Information collection. *Connecticut College, Shain Library*

Figure 4.3. Government Information collection. *Connecticut College, Shain Library*

Some of the advantages of ordering from vendors include discount pricing and the opportunity to create a back order, cancellation, and processing profile. Vendors can provide such value-added services (VAS) as processing a book to be delivered shelf ready including MARC records, barcodes, spine labels, and book covers. Each of these items incurs a small fee, but the added cost can far outweigh the time it takes to do the processing in-house. Free delivery is often available, although it may require a minimum number of books in a specific order.

The advantages to using a vendor include:

- They maintain a large inventory of titles in appropriate formats.
- They offer steep discounts on trade materials.
- They provide prompt and accurate order fulfillment.
- They provide prompt and accurate reporting (of out-of-stock or backordered items, for example).
- They provide personal service at reasonable prices.
- They provide prompt technical support for shared technology.
- They provide timely correction of faulty services (such as damaged materials).
- They provide value-added services, such as processing a book to be delivered shelf ready including MARC records, barcodes, spine labels, and book covers.

Baker & Taylor and Ingram are among the most well-known vendors, with Follet, BWI, YBP, and ebrary not far behind, particularly for schools and academic libraries. All offer processing (including book covers, barcodes, and MARC records for print materials) for a fee. (As of April 2016 Follett Corporation acquired Baker & Taylor; B&T is expected to continue to operate as before.)[6]

There is another way to acquire materials, particularly best sellers, besides purchasing them. A library may choose to lease popular print titles or multiple copies from a program offered by McNaughton (a division of Brodart, primarily a library supply vendor that also offers collection development services). This allows libraries to choose titles on a rotating basis to augment their collection or to add multiple copies for popular titles. As with the other vendors, a lease program provides the same benefits, such as the selection of specific titles, standard cataloging and processing, and free shipping. This is also a practical option for libraries with limited budgets, as they are not paying for the book but merely leasing it. This is a great way to add popular titles without committing the funds to buy something that will only be popular for a limited time. This model also allows the library to purchase the item at the end of its lease for a much lower price.[7]

There are alternatives to using a vendor such as ordering directly from the publisher, although the discount would be lower and no other services may be offered. In some cases that is necessary, though, for a specialized topic or an obscure publisher. Not to be overlooked either is your local bookstore. While the LSS is not likely to do all of the ordering through them, they are a great resource for last-minute or supplementary purchases. It is also a good idea to create a relationship with your bookseller and partner with them for author signings, book promotions, and other programs. Your discount won't be as deep as that of a vendor but the advantages of such a partnership can be quite valuable. A local library in the next town works with their local bookstore to create a wish tree in December. The library decorates the tree with paper ornaments with desired book titles on them; the bookstore sells them to patrons at a discount, who in turn donate them to the library.

ACQUISITION PROCEDURES

Print

There are also various methods of **acquisition**:

- The firm order is a list of titles the library knows it wants to order—this is considered a *micro selection*.
- The standing order is an open order for the library to receive everything on a particular topic or category (for example, annual editions of certain reference materials).
  - A variation on this is when a library chooses to receive all titles of particular authors as they are published in fiction, nonfiction, or both.
- The approval plan is when the library is sent a selection of titles from which it may choose, with the understanding that they can be returned.
  - The last two are referred to as *macro selection*, which adds large quantities of materials through mass buying plans, not by individual titles.[8]

Now let's look at the process itself. (As discussed in chapter 3, bibliographic verification of the item is the critical first step.)

Most orders are done electronically through the vendor, but it is first necessary to establish a profile detailing your preferences, such as using Dewey or LC cataloging, generating barcodes, covering books, and so on. The library needs to establish a back order and cancellation policy in their vendor profile as well (for example, an item will stay on order for twelve months; after that the order will be canceled). The procedure is similar for all formats or media. This only has to be done once; all orders will then be processed accordingly.

The vendor's website will have templates to be filled out with the ISBN and quantity of each title to be ordered. The site allows for checking incorrect or missing information and duplication of titles. When the template has been verified for correctness, the order is then submitted.

Nonprint

The focus so far has been on books; in general the process is similar for **nonprint** materials. It may be done by the same department as print materials, or by another department in a large public or academic library. The procedures would be the same, particularly bibliographic verification of the item.

The sources of nonprint items may differ. E-books, as discussed earlier, are either purchased individually or made available through a subscription to a service such as Overdrive. Individual books on CD and/or MP3 formats as well as DVD or Blu-Ray titles can be purchased through vendors as well. Some of the recommended vendors for audio and video media include:

- Advanced Educational Products (AEP)
- Alliance Entertainment
- Audio Editions
- Baker & Taylor Entertainment
- Findaway World
- Ingram Library Services
- Midwest Tape
- TEI Landmark Audio
- MicroMarketing
- Tantor Media

Gifts and Exchange

Another method of acquisition is known as **Gifts and Exchange**.

- Gifts can be those materials actively sought by the library to fill needs in the collection.
- Unsolicited materials given to the library also fall into this category. They may be useful to the collection or may be returned to the donor or used for other purposes, such as a book sale. The library needs a clearly worded policy on what gifts it accepts and their eventual disposition. No strings can be attached to a gift that would preclude the library using the gift as it sees fit.
- Exchange is the method some libraries, principally academic libraries, use to offer unused or no longer needed materials to another institution in exchange for something that fills a need in their collection.

Outsourcing

Outsourcing is yet another way that libraries can acquire materials, by contracting with a service that does the selection and processing without input from the staff. This can take the entire acquisition function out of the library altogether and may be an option for small libraries that lack trained staff to make these decisions, or for large libraries that choose to put their energy into other functions. It can be argued that this is both a time and money saver for a given library, but it is not without its detractors.

PDA/DDA/UDA

In chapter 3 we introduced the phrase "just in time, not just in case." This means that the library chooses to collect materials that patrons want to use right now, rather than hold on to older items that may not be used for the foreseeable future, if at all. Aligning to this concept is **patron-driven acquisition**, alternatively known as **demand-driven acquisition** or **use-driven acquisition**. A "just in time" tool, it goes beyond a patron requesting a particular book that the library would buy, or provide through interlibrary loan.

The 80/20 philosophy asserts that 80 percent of library circulation comes from only 20 percent of the items. That accounts for a lot of materials not being used!

Libraries are thus trying to downsize their physical collections in favor of allowing patrons to choose what materials they want or need, mostly in an electronic format. To do this, librarians choose a pool of titles that patrons could potentially want, in print or e-book. Once a patron selects a title, it is either automatically purchased or leased, and the library assumes the cost. Lynn Wiley at the University of Illinois library describes UDA as

> Controlled collection management where the user "buys":
>
> - librarians pick the pool of titles that users could potentially request. The format could be a print book in stock or an e-Book
> - The pool the vendor offers may include all the book content that could be loaded
> - or just a selection using price, copyright year, publisher and or subject to narrow selections down
> - or just newly published based on a profile set up by a vendor
> - Or a combination of these.[9]

It may include full text or selected page views. Short-term loans may also be offered. Not all titles are available as UDA, and the publisher decides what can be sold. Some items are embargoed if they are too new.

According to Elizabeth Hansen, director of information resources at the Shain Library at Connecticut College,[10] the vendor (they use YBP) works with the publishers on a license agreement that allows the library to load selected titles into their catalog without purchasing them. A profile is established with the vendor that includes such parameters as languages, academic levels, and subject areas. (Textbooks are not allowed.) A bibliographic record is loaded into the library's catalog, and if a student clicks on that link he or she will get the content and the library will be charged. Alternatively, a patron can browse for ten minutes and the library will only be charged a short-term loan fee. The criteria, or triggers, that determine the cost include the browsing time, page views, and downloads. The publishers may not make all titles available, however, and they may set limits such as not including any images. Some titles may have to be mediated, or approved by the library, before they can be accessed.

The cost of this service is included in the library's budget, and individual books cannot exceed $200. DDA/PDA provides additional content for the user and gives them a say in what goes into their library's collection. Ms. Hansen was cautiously optimistic about the use of DDA and its role in the academic library, but like technologies that have come before, there are still issues that need to be resolved—including the fact that if mostly e-books are added through DDA, there is less physical processing to be done in-house. This has an impact on the technical services department.

According to the Association of College and Research Libraries,

> It is best to view PDA as a tool amongst several to augment a library's collection development policy. User selection serves to facilitate the immediate and short-term demands of developing a collection within niches; yet the requisite foresight required to refine a comprehensive collection for future scholarship and address ongoing subject trends

necessitates the continued role of librarians in advancing an inclusive strategy. Mutually beneficial, PDA bespeaks the appreciation libraries express for the user as a valued partner. A cost-effective and customer-service oriented policy, PDA remains an evolving strategy with a demonstrated history of success.[11]

RECEIVING

Once the order is placed, the next step is to prepare for its receipt. When the shipment comes, there is a procedure to follow:

1. Unpack the boxes.
2. Find the packing slip (the actual invoice is almost always sent separately).
3. Check the packing slip against the contents—item for item.
4. Check the shipment itself against the order form to make sure what was received was what was ordered, and vice versa.

There could be problems with the shipment, including:

- Missing items
- Duplicate items
- Incorrect format (book instead of CD, large print instead of regular)
- Damage (missing pages, broken binding, cover upside down, or incorrect spine label)
- Missing copies of volumes within a set
- Incorrect prices, discounts, or VAS indicated on the packing slip

If there are problems, then the vendor must be contacted immediately: be prepared to give the order number, account number, or whatever other information they request. Most likely they will issue a return authorization number (RTA) to allow an item to be returned; there may also be a return label in the enclosed paperwork.

Once it all checks out, the materials can be processed (as needed) and properly marked. Be sure this is all done *before paying the invoice*, as materials may not be returnable unless a mistake was the vendor's error.

CHAPTER SUMMARY

This chapter on acquisitions gives us an overview of the publishing industry, including the different kinds of publishers from mainstream to electronic. The concept of vendors is introduced as well as the services they provide and the advantages of using them. This is followed by information on various methods of acquisitions of a variety of materials, formats, and sources, and the process of receiving these materials once purchased. The latest concepts of demand-driven acquisitions (DDA) or patron-driven acquisitions (PDA) are covered as well.

DISCUSSION QUESTIONS

1. Explain what a publisher does, and the difference among several kinds of publishers.
2. What is the difference between a vanity or subsidized press, and self-published books as we know them today?
3. What are the various ways a library can provide digital content to its patrons?
4. A profile has been set up with the vendor about how materials should be processed and shipped so you confidently place an order. What could go wrong?
5. PDA/DDA/UDA is a fairly recent development in academic acquisitions. How do you feel about taking some of the control away from staff and giving it to patrons? Do you envision it becoming routine in public libraries as well?

ACTIVITIES

1. Provide definitions for the following terms: publisher, vendor, and jobber. List at least one example of an organization or company in each of these categories. Visit their websites and describe one service you found to be distinctive/creative in regard to acquisitions services the company offers.
2. What criteria might be used in choosing vendors, publishers, and jobbers for library resources? Are the same criteria used in choosing each?
3. Summarize how the publishing industry has changed in recent years. Include a discussion of how e-books and self-publishing models affect a library. Describe how a library is responding to new trends in the publishing industry.

NOTES

1. "About University Presses," Association of American University Presses, last modified 2015, accessed January 11, 2016, http://www.aaupnet.org/about-aaup/about-university-presses.

2. G. Edward Evans, Sheila S. Intner, and Jean Weihs, *Introduction to Technical Services*, 8th ed., Library and Information Science Text Series (Santa Barbara, CA: Libraries Unlimited, 2011), 134.

3. "booklife," *Publishers Weekly*, accessed January 12, 2016, http://www.publishersweekly.com/pw/diy/index.html.

4. "Higginson Book Company," Higginson Book Company, accessed January 12, 2016, http://www.higginsonbooks.com/index.html.

5. "Google Books Library Project—An enhanced card catalog of the world's books," Google, accessed January 12, 2016, https://www.google.com/googlebooks/library/.

6. Matt Enis, "Follett Acquires Baker & Taylor," *Library Journal*, last modified April 18, 2016, accessed May 15, 2016, http://lj.libraryjournal.com/2016/04/ed-tech/follett-acquires-baker-taylor.

7. "McNaughton Adult Lease," Brodart, accessed January 13, 2016, http://www.brodartbooks.com/mcnaughton-library-subscription-services/adult/page.aspx?id=270.

8. George M. Eberhart, ed., *The Whole Library Handbook*, 5th ed. (Chicago, IL: ALA, 2013), 248.

9. Lynn Wiley, "PDA DDA It's all AOK!?," Consortium of Academic and Research Libraries in Illinois (CARLI), last modified June 2, 2014, accessed January 10, 2016, http://www.carli.illinois.edu/sites/files/coll_man/Wiley_PDA_DDA.pdf.

10. Elizabeth Hansen, interview by the author, Shain Library, Connecticut College, New London, CT, January 13, 2016.

11. Stephen Arougheti, "Keeping Up with . . . Patron Driven Acquisitions," Association of College and Research Libraries, accessed January 10, 2016, http://www.ala.org/acrl/publications/keeping_up_with/pda.

REFERENCES, SUGGESTED READINGS, AND WEBSITES

Arougheti, Stephen. "Keeping Up with . . . Patron Driven Acquisitions." Association of College and Research Libraries. Accessed January 10, 2016. http://www.ala.org/acrl/publications/keeping_up_with/pda.

Association of American University Presses. "About University Presses." Association of American University Presses. Last modified 2015. Accessed January 11, 2016. http://www.aaupnet.org/about-aaup/about-university-presses.

Brewer, Robert Lee. "The Writer's Dig." *Writer's Digest*. Last modified April 23, 2014. Accessed January 11, 2016. http://www.writersdigest.com/online-editor/the-pros-and-cons-of-publishing-with-a-small-publisher.

Brodart Books & Library Services. "McNaughton Adult Lease." Brodart. Accessed January 13, 2016. http://www.brodartbooks.com/mcnaughton-library-subscription-services/adult/page.aspx?id=270.

Brown, Alanna. "Why Indie Publishing Beats a Mainstream Book Deal." *Huffington Post*. Last modified July 9, 2013. Accessed January 11, 2016. http://www.huffingtonpost.com/luxeco-living/why-indie-publishing-beat_b_3563203.html.

Chadwick, Cynthia, Renee DiPilato, Monique LeConge, Rachel Rubin, and Gary Shaffer. "The Future of the FDLP in Public Libraries." Public Libraries Online. Last modified December 26, 2012. Accessed January 15, 2016. http://publiclibrariesonline.org/2012/10/the-future-of-the-fdlp-in-public-libraries/.

Enis, Matt. "Follett Acquires Baker & Taylor." *Library Journal*. Last modified April 18, 2016. Accessed May 15, 2016. http://lj.libraryjournal.com/2016/04/ed-tech/follett-acquires-baker-taylor/#_.

Evans, G. Edward, Sheila S. Intner, and Jean Weihs. *Introduction to Technical Services*. 8th ed. Library and Information Science Text Series. Santa Barbara, CA: Libraries Unlimited, 2011.

Google. "Google Books Library Project—An Enhanced Card Catalog of the World's Books." Google. Accessed January 12, 2016. https://www.google.com/googlebooks/library/.

Hansen, Elizabeth. Interview by the author. Shain Library, Connecticut College, New London, CT. January 13, 2016.

Higginson Book Company. "Higginson Book Company." Higginson Book Company. Accessed January 12, 2016. http://www.higginsonbooks.com/index.html.

Junior Library Guild. "How JLG Works." Junior Library Guild. Last modified 2016. Accessed January 14, 2016. http://www.juniorlibraryguild.com/how-jlg-works/.

Miller, William. "Patron-Driven Acquisition (PDA): The New Wave in Book Acquisitions Is Coming." *Library Issues* 31, no. 5 (May 2011).

Publishers Weekly. "booklife." Accessed January 12, 2016. http://www.publishersweekly.com/pw/diy/index.html.

Science Fiction and Fantasy Writers of America. "Vanity/Subsidy Publishers." SFWA. Last modified December 30, 2014. Accessed January 12, 2016. http://www.sfwa.org/other-re-sources/for-authors/writer-beware/vanity/.

Wiley, Lynn. "PDA DDA It's All AOK!?" Consortium of Academic and Research Libraries in Illinois (CARLI). Last modified June 2, 2014. Accessed January 10, 2016. http://www.carli.illinois.edu/sites/files/coll_man/Wiley_PDA_DDA.pdf.

CHAPTER 5

Collection Management

LSS know the basic principles of collection development and management. (ALA-LSSC Competency #2)

Topics Covered in This Chapter:

- Collection Promotion
  - Marketing
  - Branding
- Shelving and Stack Maintenance
  - Elements of Shelving
    - Shelf Reading
    - Collection Shifting
- Digital Collection Management

Key Terms:

Branding: Branding is the process involved in creating a unique name and image for a product in the consumer's mind, through advertising campaigns with a consistent theme. This is an effective tool to promote the library's collection.

Collection promotion: Collection promotion is the activity that LSS perform to advertise or highlight what the library has to offer in their print and digital collections. It can be done in-house with displays and promotions, or through outreach to traditional and social media.

Digital materials: Digital materials are those that are not in print or book form. In a library they can consist of research databases, electronic serials or journals, electronic books, audiobooks, and streaming content. They are an important element of a library collection but may have issues of access and cost.

Marketing: Marketing is the process of promoting a service to a target audience. Libraries routinely market collections, services, and programs to bring users into the library to increase their use.

Shelf reading: Shelf reading describes the process of physically going along a row of books to make sure they are in the correct order, either alphabetically or by call number. This ensures that items are where they are supposed to be in order to be easily located.

Shifting: Collection shifting is an ongoing task to perform to avoid shelves getting too tight—that is, having so many books jammed in that it is often impossible to pull a single item off the shelf. This creates a more inviting look and enables the browser to find materials more easily.

COLLECTION PROMOTION

In previous chapters we were introduced to the functions of collection development, including selection policies, demographics, and acquisitions. Now that we have a library full of terrific resources—targeted to our users—what do we do about getting them to circulate or be used in-house for reference and research? How do we let our patrons and community know what the library has to offer? This is where **collection promotion** comes in.

First of all, libraries are many things to many people in a community. They offer:

- Books—print and electronic
- Media—books on CD or MP3, DVDs, and Blu-Ray
- Periodicals: print and electronic on a multitude of topics
- Databases: health, education, business, computers, job search
- Services: Internet access, copiers, fax machines, databases

No matter how good a collection is, it is useless if no one uses it. It is necessary to get the word out about what your facility has in its collection that will benefit the public.

Marketing

Marketing has to be part of any library's promotion. Besides wanting to bring attention to collections and services, libraries are in competition with so many other options, including bookstores, portable e-readers, and the Internet. There are those, of course, who predict the end of libraries, but we are finding that they are still relevant both as a place to find information, materials, and services, and as the "third place"—the social area separate from home and work. People are living increasingly more isolated lives, as evidenced by the explosion of social networking. The library provides a physical space they may otherwise lack.

For library collections, marketing is based on the effort to discover, create, and satisfy customer needs. It relies on designing the library's offerings in terms of the needs and desires of the library's demographic, and on using effective communication to inform and motivate. Libraries have been slow to come to the marketing table. After all, we're libraries and everyone knows what we do, right? Libraries have changed so much that it is no longer good enough to rest on our former reputation. If we don't let the public know what we are about these days, who will?

There are many effective ways to promote a library's collection. The print media campaign is still a useful tool for promoting the library's collection. This means sharing your information with as many media outlets as you can identify, including:

- Newspapers
- Radio stations
- Cable television stations
- Radio public service announcements
- Library newsletters

One can also use the library's (print or electronic) mailing lists of patrons, book groups, and even other libraries to let them know what is being highlighted at any given time. For those of us still addicted to print, getting an automated message or e-mail from the library that a requested book has come in *and is being held just for you*, is incentive enough to run right over.

Social media is an invaluable marketing tool as well. Facebook, blogs, Twitter, Instagram, Tumblr, e-mail, and texts are great tools to get the word out, particularly these days when most people are constantly connected to their mobile devices. Libraries have a diverse clientele, and it's up to the library to recognize this and then get the word out in the most appropriate way for each group.

Part of the marketing strategy includes displays. Think of the grocery or drug store: magazines and candy displayed at the checkout, and aisle endcap displays of sales and specials. By highlighting inventory and making it available the store draws attention to something it wants you to buy. These items are displayed for precisely that reason. The same can be true in the library. There are different kinds of signage and displays with different purposes:

- Directional signage can provide a floor plan and a guide to the rooms within the library, such as the reference, children's, or rest rooms.
- Location indicators on shelving can direct the patron to the content of the collection and can also be used to cross-reference parts of the collection.
- Displays can highlight new materials, topics of interest, or current events both in and out of the library.

The opportunity exists for any number of special displays—thematically linked to a holiday, season, or subject.

Branding

Another way to increase your visibility is by branding. **Branding** is not the same as marketing; rather, it is an important first step and part of the "marketing mix." Branding is part of the marketing *strategy*, while promotion and publicity are part of the marketing *tools*.[1] Branding is the process involved in creating a unique name and image for a product in the consumers' mind, through advertising campaigns with a consistent theme. Branding aims to establish a presence in the market that attracts and retains loyal customers. It's making your library known for something.

Branding your library raises its visibility in its community, which serves to increase its use. Examples that have been used in libraries across the country include: *Browsing Is Just the Beginning; Something to Believe In; Discovery Begins Here;* and *A World of Possibility.* They serve as "hooks" to get the attention of their communities. Marketing and branding serve as excellent promotion for your library's collection and services—and after all, isn't that what collection promotion is all about?[2]

SHELVING AND STACK MAINTENANCE

Elements of Shelving

Items that need to be **shelved** include new acquisitions, returned circulating materials, and items used in-house. Shelving is often the responsibility of the LSS, and sometimes pages or volunteers. We discourage patron reshelving of items they have used in the library in order to avoid shelving mistakes. An item shelved in the wrong place may as well be lost.

Those who shelve should be given instruction on how to do so; for volunteers, a tutorial is often called for. As an example of how this can be helpful, a library director related the story of a woman who had been volunteering in her public library for quite a while and who appeared to understand the instructions. That is, until one day, as part of a conversation about shelving, she turned to this director and said "You mean they're alphabetical?"

For books, fiction titles in Dewey Decimal Classification (DDC) are arranged on the shelf in alphabetical order by author. Multiple books by one author would then be arranged alphabetically by title within that author regardless of publication date. An example would be textbox 5.1, titles by author Alafair Burke. In Library of Congress (LC) classification, fiction is a little trickier, as all literature, including fiction, falls under PS. The numbers then follow in order, as shown in the Asimov titles in textbox 5.2.

Fiction titles that begin with a number always come first (*212*); and the initial articles *A, An,* or *The* are ignored in the alphabetization. This is why *The Cinderella Murder* in textbox 5.1 looks out of place but is actually not. However, beware of yet another potential trap: there may be other authors with the same last name! Make sure all of Alafair Burke's titles are filed correctly under *her* name, and not interfiled with those of her father, James Burke. This is a very common error made in shelving; it's not enough to just read the spine label, so take the book in hand to make sure all of the information is correct, including the author.

The same problem involves multiple authors with the same last name such as Carol Higgins Clark, Mary Higgins Clark, and Arthur C. Clarke. If the spine label only uses the first three letters of the last name, CLA, then it is not only possible but probable that the works of all three of these authors with be interfiled alphabetically

TEXTBOX 5.1 TITLES IN ALPHABETICAL ORDER REGARDLESS OF PUBLICATION DATE, DDC

BUR	*212* (2010)
BUR	*All Day and a Night* (2014)
BUR	*Angel's Tip* (2008)
BUR	*The Cinderella Murder*
BUR	*Close Case* (2005)
BUR	*Dead Connection* (2007)
BUR	*If You Were Here* (2013)
BUR	*Judgment Calls* (2003)
BUR	*Long Gone* (2011)
BUR	*Missing Justice* (2004)
BUR	*Never Tell* (2012)

TEXTBOX 5.2 TITLES IN ALPHABETICAL ORDER REGARDLESS OF PUBLICATION DATE, LC

PS3551.S5 F35 1966	*Fantastic Voyage*, Isaac Asimov (1966)
PS3551.S5 F5 1951	*Foundation*, Isaac Asimov (1951)
PS3551.S5 F6 1982	*Foundation's Edge*, Isaac Asimov (1982)

if carelessly shelved. Even if the entire last name is on the spine label, it can still happen. In my library, Arthur Clarke's final "e" contributed to shelving problems.

Nonfiction is arranged by call number, and then alphabetically by author within the call number range. The items may share the same call number, but then the titles are alphabetical by the author. The following textbox shows books on Asian cooking as they should be arranged on the shelf.

The exception is if an author happens to have several titles in one subject category or call number, then the third step is to arrange by title.

Like items are usually shelved together: books with books, CDs with CDs, and so on. Some libraries choose to interfile all items by the same author together on the shelf. This allows a patron to find everything by a particular author or subject side by side on the shelf, regardless of format. The examples given in textboxes 5.1–5.4

TEXTBOX 5.3 TITLES IN CALL NUMBER ORDER, DDC

641.595 HAI	Hair, Jaden	*Steamy Kitchen*
641.595 MEE	Meehan, Peter	*101 Easy Asian Recipes*
641.595 WAN	Wang, Yuan	*Ancient Wisdom, Modern Kitchen*

TEXTBOX 5.4 TITLES IN CALL NUMBER ORDER, LC

TX715.C57424 1999	Spaulding, Lily Mae	*Civil War Recipes: Receipts from the Pages of Godey's Lady's Book*
TX715.F684 2014	Veit, Helen Zoe	*Food in the Civil War Era: The North*
TX715.F685 2015	Veit, Helen Zoe	*Food in the Civil War Era: The South*

apply as well to the shelving or interfiling of multiple formats. It would be easy to be casual or careless about this, but it is *not* OK to mix them all up! Materials that are incorrectly shelved may as well be lost—and that does nothing for collection promotion.

Another thing to remember about shelving is that if books cannot be shelved upright, they should be shelved on their "backs" with the spine down. Shelving with the spine up can actually damage or break the spine. This is especially true with oversized books.

Shelf Reading

An important part of the shelving routine involves **shelf reading**. Just as it sounds, the LSS would look at a shelf of books and "read" the row of call numbers. Each

Figure 5.1. Right way to shelve a book. *Bill Memorial Library*

Figure 5.2. Wrong way to shelve a book. *Bill Memorial Library*

item needs to be taken off the shelf to examine the full author name and title, as that cannot always be determined by the call number.

When shelving or shelf reading, check the three books on either side of the one being shelved or read, as well as the shelves above and below. This means that the three on either side may be in order so seven books are in perfect order. However— the shelf above or below may contain another few books by the same author, also in perfect order. By checking the end of one shelf or the beginning of another, the LSS can be sure all of that author's books are in the correct placement.

Another component here is called reader interest shelving. Using this method, the LSS can group materials together by genre. Examples of the most popular kinds of reader interest shelving include mysteries, romances, science fiction, or westerns. (This list is not inclusive of all possibilities.) Titles that fit this category may get a specially identifiable sticker put on their spines so they can be identified and thus can be shelved together, isolated from the rest of the collection. Another option is to interfile those genres, because as long as they have their special sticker they can be easily identified from the rest of the collection.

There are pros and cons to this kind of practice. Some authors may be considered mystery writers in one library but not in another. What may be a "mystery novel" to one patron may not be to another, or to the LSS. A patron could go directly to the mystery section and end up walking away empty-handed if, for example, he was looking for something by Dick Francis. Not finding it there, he may assume the

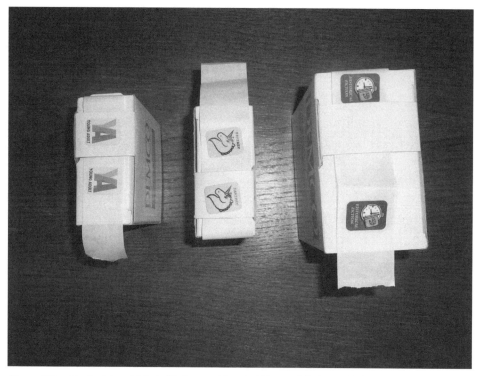

Figure 5.3.   Reader interest labels: YA, Fantasy, Historical Fiction. *Bill Memorial Library*

library did not have it when in fact it did, as this particular library doesn't identify Francis as a mystery author and the book would be located on the "regular" fiction shelf. In this situation, inter-shelving all mysteries alphabetically by author within the larger collection would avoid that problem. There are a couple of advantages to this: it can actually free up shelf space, as creating special areas can take up space; and patrons may find new authors and genres by not limiting their searching to only one area.

Collection Shifting

Collection shifting is an ongoing task to perform to avoid shelves getting too tight—that is, having so many books jammed in that it is often impossible to pull a single item off the shelf. If you've ever browsed the shelves in a library and found items lying on top of a shelf, it could be for two reasons—a library patron didn't know where to put it back or the shelf is so crowded that it cannot fit. Ideally a shelf should have about two fists worth of space at the end of each shelf. This allows for some expansion, or even to display an item.

But when the shelf is so full that not another book can be shelved, then it's time to shift. Ultimately the collection is shifted to afford more space. Look through all the shelves to see if they are all crowded or if several areas have a lot of space at the

Figure 5.4. Shifted shelves before (below) and after (above). *Bill Memorial Library*

end of the row. In that case books can be moved from the end of one shelf to the beginning of the next one—provided that the next shelf also has extra room.

In some cases an entire section will be too tight. This can involve finding space elsewhere in the collection and working backward or forward to move books around to get the right mix. It can be frustrating and tiring, as lifting volumes for a long period of time can take its toll. Sometimes the reality is that there is no space left to shift anything. In that case the LSS should consider weeding the collection to make more space as well as withdrawing materials that are no longer essential to hold on to. Chapter 6 will cover the topics of inventory and weeding in detail.

DIGITAL COLLECTION MANAGEMENT

Some of the same concerns about management of a print collection apply as well to a digital collection. "E-books should be treated in the same way as physical collections, with retention based on use, accuracy of information, and relevance to the patron."[3] Librarians must justify what they purchase, and must look closely at what is being requested and used. As we saw in chapter 4, electronic publishing has provided us with relatively easy access to textbooks, serials, and e-books. The difference in the management of digital materials is that access to electronic content may require subscriptions, fees, and special devices, and there may be some limited use restrictions.

Libraries must pay for licenses or subscription fees when purchasing digital content. "An additional concern with e-books is ongoing and future costs. Since the information contained in e-books is stored on a publisher or vendor's server, many of them charge annually for continued access to the platform. Even though the library has paid for the digital item, it must pay an additional fee to ensure that patrons can use the platform to access the content."[4] In other words, a library may be charged a per-use fee in addition to the fees paid to subscribe. Libraries cannot archive any of this material, either, as they never owned it. Agreements usually allow for printing as long as it is not in violation of copyright laws.

If print materials are lost or damaged, the LSS can request a copy through interlibrary loan from any number of libraries that also own it. With digital materials, "what happens when the library no longer subscribes to or can pay for the platform through which the e-resource is accessed by patrons? What happens if the publisher or supplier of the e-resource ceases to exist? What happens as software develops and the technology used to access a book's content is no longer supported?"[5] This is not a new concern—how many computers today have drives for floppy disks? Technology changes so rapidly that formats in use today may be obsolete in the not-too-distant future.

Solutions to the cost issue can include libraries partnering with one another to cooperatively share databases. Many states contract with vendors to create a database with a wide variety of content. For a relatively low subscription fee, libraries all over the state can offer free access to informational resources for students of all ages including databases, newspapers, magazines, scholarly journals, and health, business, biographical, and genealogy sites. Individual libraries can choose to buy into additional databases as needed.

Most library subscriptions or license fees, which can cost several thousands of dollars, are for a specific period of time, usually one year. The reasons for this may be that only annual contracts are allowed if the library is tax supported, such as public and school libraries. A shorter license period allows for libraries to modify their agreements if needed.[6] Costs may also change based on population fluctuation if the subscription model charges per population or user, typical of academic libraries.

Some may argue that digital collections are cheaper than paper and take up less space, but the subscription costs and fees must be carefully considered in the maintenance of a digital collection.

CHAPTER SUMMARY

Collection management can have several meanings, one of them being synonymous with collection development, which we dealt with in chapter 2. In this case it means the actual physical maintenance of the collection, both print and digital. It includes shelving and shifting materials, and shelf reading for accuracy. It means promoting the collection to be sure that your community knows what your library offers, and in which formats. Marketing brings attention to your library, and branding improves its profile, or visibility, in the community. Collection management of both print and digital materials is an essential function to assure that library users, in all kinds of libraries, have access to current materials in their choice of format in a timely manner.

DISCUSSION QUESTIONS

1. What are some of the elements of collection maintenance?
2. How can a library promote its collection?
3. Explain the difference between marketing and branding; give examples.
4. Explain the importance of shelf reading and collection shifting.
5. Give the pros and cons of maintaining a digital collection.

ACTIVITIES

1. Prepare a bibliography with brief notations of five articles that identify the effectiveness of marketing as a promotion tool.
2. Schedule an interview with a librarian involved in digital collections. How does she/he determine what materials are purchased or subscribed to, including databases, serials, and e-books?

NOTES

1. Elisabeth Doucette, "Branding for Public Libraries," *Lyrasis*, last modified December 8, 2009, accessed February 5, 2015, http://www.slideshare.net/conniemassey/branding-for-public-libraries.

2. Hali R. Keeler, *Foundations of Library Service*, Library Support Staff Handbooks 1 (Lanham, MD: Rowman & Littlefield, 2015), 158–61.

3. Alene E. Moroni, "Weeding in a Digital Age," *Library Journal* 137, no. 15 (September 15, 2012): 26–28, accessed January 22, 2016, http://search.ebscohost.com/login.aspx?direct=true&db=aph&AN=80445399&authtype=cookie,cpid&custid=s1024272&site=ehost-live&scope=site.

4. Kathleen A. Lehman, "Collection Development and Management," Library Resources & Technical Services, last modified July 2014, accessed January 22, 2016, http://search.ebscohost.com/login.aspx?direct=true&db=aph&AN=97294511&authtype=cookie,cpid&custid=s1024272&site=ehost-live&scope=site.

5. Ibid.

6. Marie Keen Shaw, *Library Technology and Digital Resources*, Library Support Staff Handbooks 2 (Lanham, MD: Rowman & Littlefield, 2015), 90.

REFERENCES, SUGGESTED READINGS, AND WEBSITES

Coffman, Steve. "What If You Ran Your Library Like a Bookstore?" *American Libraries* 29, no. 3 (March 1998): 40. https://search.ebscohost.com/login.aspx?direct=true&db=aph&AN=306538&site=ehost-live&scope=site.

Doucette, Elisabeth. "Branding for Public Libraries." *Lyrasis*. Last modified December 8, 2009. Accessed February 5, 2015. http://www.slideshare.net/conniemassey/branding-for-public-libraries.

Keeler, Hali R. *Foundations of Library Service*. Library Support Staff Handbooks 1. Lanham, MD: Rowman & Littlefield, 2015.

Lehman, Kathleen A. "Collection Development and Management." Library Resources & Technical Services. Last modified July 2014. Accessed January 22, 2016. http://search.ebscohost.com/login.aspx?direct=true&db=aph&AN=97294511&authtype=cookie,cpid&custid=s1024272&site=ehost-live&scope=site.

"Library Digital Collection: Getting Started." Video file. YouTube. Posted by Overdrive, April 22, 2013. Accessed January 23, 2016. https://www.youtube.com/watch?v=CUuJWQTGj8o.

Moody, Kim. "Covert Censorship in Libraries: A Discussion Paper." Reading, 2005.

Moroni, Alene E. "Weeding in a Digital Age." *Library Journal* 137, no. 15 (September 15, 2012): 26–28. Accessed January 22, 2016. http://search.ebscohost.com/login.aspx?direct=true&db=aph&AN=80445399&authtype=cookie,cpid&custid=s1024272&site=ehost-live&scope=site.

OCLC. "ContentDM." OCLC. Last modified 2016. Accessed January 22, 2016. http://www.oclc.org/en-US/contentdm/features.html.

Shaw, Marie Keen. *Library Technology and Digital Resources*. Library Support Staff Handbooks 2. Lanham, MD: Rowman & Littlefield, 2015.

CHAPTER 6

Inventory and Deselection

LSS assist with decisions regarding selection, deselection, retention and replacement of all types of library resources. (ALA-LSSC Competency #3)

Topics Covered in This Chapter:

- Inventorying the Print Collection
- Deselection, or "Weeding" the Collection
  - Policy and Criteria
  - The Process
- CREW Method of Deselection
  - Disposition of Deselected Items
- Deselection of Electronic Items

Key Terms:

CREW: CREW stands for Continuous Revision Evaluation Weeding. First created in 1976, it is a method that provides guidelines for evaluating, and ultimately deselecting, materials from a library collection. It is a manual that has been updated and expanded to keep pace with modern standards and technology.

Deselection: Deselection, also known as weeding, means to cull, or withdraw from the collection, materials that are outdated and no longer useful. The justification for deselection is to maintain a collection that is vital, relevant, and useful. It should be a part of an overall collection development policy and is a continuous process.

Inventory: An inventory is a complete listing of the items in a collection. Physically inventorying a library collection means that every item in the collection will be examined to assess its status, including its placement on the shelf, its cataloging, and its use or circulation activity.

Shelf list: The term "shelf list" refers to the practice of having a master list of every item in the library held apart from the regular catalog. It is used to compare library holdings to actual items. Previously done with catalog cards, most shelf lists are now held electronically in a database.

In chapters 2 and 3 we learned about collection development and the selection of materials for both print and digital collections. In this chapter we will now learn about taking a good look at what's in the collection and how, or if, items should be kept or withdrawn. If that sounds counterproductive, it is actually not. As it has been said before, no library can have everything; cooperative collection, interlibrary loan, and PDA are all ways to get items to people that the library does not own.

Even so, there comes a time in every library, no matter how large or small, public, school or academic, that there is simply no more room to put another item on the shelf. As tempting as it would be to simply go up and down the aisles tossing books that don't fit, this process must begin by doing a complete inventory of the collections, both print and digital.

INVENTORYING THE PRINT COLLECTION

Inventory is the *ongoing* process of comparing the "shelf list" of the library holdings to actual items. The term "shelf list" comes from the practice of having catalog cards for every item. Usually a set of catalog cards would be produced for each item: a shelf list card, an author entry, a title entry, and a subject entry. While the author, title, and subject cards would be interfiled in the card catalog for public searching, the shelf list card was kept in its own, separate card catalog in the librarian's office or the technical service area. This served as a master list of everything held by the library. Few libraries do so today, instead using the electronic catalog from the online library system for this purpose.

Physically inventorying the collection makes the assumption that every item in the collection, at some time, will be examined by a real person. In doing a physical exam of a collection item by item, the LSS is also assessing the status of everything collection related, including each item's placement on the shelf, its cataloging, and its use or circulation activity.

Performing an inventory is a labor-intensive task and is usually not done all at once. Like shelf reading or any other maintenance activity, the library must integrate inventory into the regular activity of managing a library collection. Inventory and deselection often go hand in hand. When the LSS is performing inventory, she needs to answer these questions:

- Is an item meeting the needs and working within the scope of the library's collection development policy?
- Is the item being used?

- Are the librarians responsible for that collection (in large or academic libraries) making the best use of budget and resources?

Performing an inventory of the collection can be overwhelming or it can be, if done regularly and methodically, very "doable" as long as the LSS sets some parameters, or limits. As the saying goes, if one looks at a project in its entirety it may seem impossible, but if taken in small parts, it is easily accomplished. For example, when inventorying adult fiction it can be as easy as deciding to do one letter of the alphabet daily (or weekly, depending on the size of the collection). Other examples include limiting nonfiction materials to all items from 001 up to 100 for one period of time. If the LSS looked at the entire children's room, for example, he might turn around and walk out—but if he chooses to begin with just picture books with the author's name starting with "A," the project is much less daunting. Doing it in small bites makes it more manageable.

The actual process involves taking the shelf list (the drawer of a card catalog, a printout of one section of the collection, or using a handheld scanner and laptop or tablet) and comparing what is on the list with what is on the shelf. Sounds easy, right? In a perfect world, everything would be in its proper place, but when doing inventory, the LSS is apt to find:

- missing books—i.e., books that are on the shelf but not in the shelf list or electronic record;
- items claimed returned by a patron but still showing up as overdue in their record;
- books that were still checked out to patrons that were shelved without being checked in;
- damaged books that need some attention;
- books that were shelved incorrectly;
- interlibrary loan materials from other libraries that were shelved rather than sent back.

DESELECTION, OR "WEEDING" THE COLLECTION

What do we mean by "deselection?" Deselection, also known as weeding, means to cull, or withdraw from the collections, materials that are outdated and no longer useful. The justification for deselection is to maintain a collection that is vital, relevant, and useful. However, libraries are experiencing increasing scrutiny from the public and funding sources, and may be required to justify their discard practices in more detail. Access to online library catalogs and direct requests for interlibrary loan may cause some librarians to hold on even more tightly to materials that should be discarded because "someone" may request the item. This brings us back to the concept of "just in time" rather than "just in case." Invariably several days after agonizing about a withdrawal, someone will come in requesting that very book—but that is the chance we have to take for the good of the collection. It can be found elsewhere to fulfill the patron's request.

Deselection is an integral part of collection development. We balance what is acquired with what needs discarding. It's not unlike the concept that some parents use at birthdays—for every new toy a child gets, one has to be given away to someone less fortunate. Systematic removal of materials that are no longer useful is essential to maintaining the quality of your collection.

As stated on the "Why We Weed" page of the website Awful Library Books (more on that later): "Weeding is an essential component of library collection management. Most libraries simply do not have unlimited space, and we must continually make room for new materials. Weeding is necessary to remain relevant to our users and true to our missions. Remember—unless your library exists to archive and preserve materials for the ages, we are not in the business of collecting physical things. We collect information and provide access to information. We love books as much as anyone and sometimes hard decisions have to be made. How many times have you said, 'But I just bought that!' and then realized it was ten years ago?"[1]

Deselection can be an emotionally difficult job as no one wants to get rid of materials, particularly if the person doing the weeding is also the person who selected it in the first place. It can feel like abandoning an old friend. For those who can do this dispassionately it may seem like an unpleasant but necessary chore. As library humor columnist Will Manley states, "Next to emptying the outdoor book drop on cold and snowy days, weeding is the most undesirable job in the library. It is also one of the most important. Collections that go unweeded tend to be cluttered, unattractive, and unreliable informational resources."[2]

TEXTBOX 6.1 BENEFITS OF DESELECTION

There are six benefits of deselection:

1. It saves space.
2. It saves time.
3. It makes the collection more appealing.
4. It increases circulation.
5. It enhances the collection's reputation for reliability.
6. It provides for feedback on collection strengths and weaknesses.

It also allows for a continuous check on condition of items for mending or repair.

Notice number 4—*weeding increases circulation*. It does so because once unneeded materials are taken off the shelf, what is left has more room and is more visible. This can be quite evident when collections are thoroughly deselected—it's as if the library had added titles instead of removed them.

Finally, academic libraries tend to move deselected items to off-site storage instead of disposing of them. This is a topic of discussion in academic libraries that are always running out of space, in that decisions must be made as to where the items go for storage, how they are shelved, and how they are retrieved when needed. There are costs involved in this process that must be taken into consideration.

Policy and Criteria

Deselection should be a part of your overall **collection development policy** and a continuous process. The policy should have wording that explains the purpose of deselection and why it is necessary. It should also explain the criteria used in choosing materials to be culled, the process for doing so, who is responsible for carrying out the process, and how these materials are disposed of. A sample policy or statement follows:

TEXTBOX 6.2 SAMPLE DESELECTION STATEMENT

Deselection: Materials that no longer meet the stated objectives of the library (including items that have become damaged or obsolete) will be systematically withdrawn according to the accepted professional practices. Disposal of withdrawn library materials will be at the discretion of the library director, subject to all relevant provisions of the Charter of the Town of _____ and the statutes of the State of _____ .

Deselection addresses these criteria:

- Contents
  - Out-of-date material that is misleading or factually inaccurate
  - Items that may have been superseded by a new edition or a better book on the subject
  - Outdated best sellers as well as books that have outlived their popularity
- Format
  - Pages that are badly soiled or torn or are missing
  - Binding may be in poor condition, beyond repair
  - Print or paper may be of such poor quality that it is difficult to read
  - Books that may have been "edited" by patrons
- Use
  - the total circulations of items on the shelf, including the last date of use
- Publication date:
  - approximately 50 percent of the circulation of a title occurs in the first five years after publication and acquisition
- Last circulation date:
  - consider removing items that have not circulated in three to five years.[3]

The Process

There is a process to follow that makes weeding logical and orderly:

1. Shelf-read first to make sure the material is in order (especially helpful if an inventory is being done as well).
2. Use the shelf list to check against what is actually there.
3. Use established guides like the Wilson series of Core Collections for whatever part of the collection you are working on: Fiction, Children's, etc. These guides indicate what titles and authors are recommended for a collection, and should stay put.
4. Arm yourself with plenty of scrap paper and a pencil to make notes about what may be missing from the shelf, may be cataloged incorrectly, or may need mending, and so on.
5. As previously noted in the section on Inventory, have the shelf list printout, drawer, or a tablet/laptop and scanner.
6. Arrange what you need on a book truck, so you have a place to put deselected items.

Once you have everything in place you are ready to start.

CREW METHOD OF DESELECTION

While the process may seem daunting, there are guidelines to follow so nothing is withdrawn arbitrarily. The easiest way to do this is by following the **CREW**[4] manual. CREW stands for **C**ontinuous **R**evision **E**valuation **W**eeding. First created in 1976 by Joseph P. Segal and Belinda Boon, it has been updated and expanded to keep pace with modern standards and technology and is a product of the Texas State Library and Archives Commission. It is the "bible" for weeding library collections and is widely used.

The criteria are clear for each type of item—fiction, nonfiction, children's, biographies, electronic, and so on.

TEXTBOX 6.3 MUSTIE

MUSTIE is an easily remembered acronym for six negative factors that ruin a book's usefulness:

M = Misleading: The item contains outdated and obsolete information in law, science, space, health and medicine, technology, travel.
U = Ugly: The book is worn out, ragged, rebound, worn, shabby, torn, dirty, yellowed, taped, missing pages.
S = Superseded: A newer edition or better book has come out to replace it.
T = Trivial: The item is of no literary or scientific value.
I = Irrelevant: The book is irrelevant to the needs of your community.
E = Elsewhere: The material may be borrowed elsewhere.

Other red flags include material that contains biased, racist, or sexist terminology or views. Weeding also helps to identify unneeded duplicates. Using the CREW manual you will see there are yet other criteria to consider: age and circulation. This means the LSS must consider the age of the book and how often it circulates.

So now we have a formula to use: AGE/CIRC/MUSTIE. CREW uses Dewey, so, for example, in the following nonfiction areas, the suggested formula is:

610 (Medicine)	5/3/MUSTIE
004 (Computers)	3/X/MUSTIE

The first number indicates the latest copyright or age of material; the second number indicates the years since it last circulated. The X means that value isn't applicable for the subject. The third field is MUSTIE, which is the final determining factor. Guidelines for specific areas are included in the CREW Manual, and materials in fast-changing fields of research, such as medicine, science, and technology, will have a 5/3/MUSTIE designation. Be assured, CREW covers all Dewey classes with specificity within the divisions as needed. It also offers the reasons behind the recommendations. In the example given for 610 (Medicine), it says "Weed ruthlessly when it comes to current medical practices. Patrons rely on up-to-date information and outdated information can be dangerous. . . . Regularly review books on fast changing topics, such as AIDS, fertility, cancer, and genetics to ensure that the information is up-to-date and accurate."[5]

The criteria for children's and YA nonfiction are the same as for adults. Be aware, however, of inaccuracy and triviality, not uncommon when an author oversimplifies information.

For adult fiction, additional considerations include whether the book is part of a series, or if the author is still writing. That is not necessarily the same as whether the author is still living, as it is well documented that death is no deterrent to some authors, such as Tom Clancy, Robert Ludlum, V. C. Andrews, and Dick Francis. Estate-approved authors can carry on their legacies, as can the occasional "suddenly discovered" or "previously unpublished" manuscript. The formula for fiction is generally X/2/MUSTIE; it is largely circulation driven.

The same formula and considerations apply for children's and YA (teen) books with the addition of abridged classics. If there is a choice, go for the unabridged edition. Physical condition is a major factor, as children's books can be well loved. Tattered books or those with broken bindings and outdated styles should be discarded, or replaced if still popular. Discard fad books (e.g., movie or TV tie-ins) as soon as the popularity has waned. Children's books can be difficult to discard because there are so many titles, classic and otherwise, that have an emotional component. Perhaps it was a favorite from your childhood, or one you read to your children over and over.

This brings us to the previously mentioned website Awful Library Books (subtitled "Hoarding Is Not Collection Development"). "This site is a collection of library holdings that we find amusing and/or questionable for libraries trying to maintain a current and relevant collection. Contained in this site are actual library holdings."[6] *My Big Sister Takes Drugs*, from 1990 is one example; *Don't Make Me Go Back, Mommy: A Child's Book about Satanic Ritual Abuse*, from 2009, is another. Admittedly many of the books are dated and may have been appropriate for their time; others are just strange. The commentary on this site, however, is priceless.

There have been several trends in reference materials. One has been to interfile reference books with the circulating collection so all materials on the same topic are in the same place. Many libraries only have small reference collections, or none at all because of all that is available online. Reference in libraries can include links in their websites to government resources, ready references, and other databases. Depending on the currency of the sites, some print-based reference materials can be eliminated entirely. Libraries will usually retain one set of an encyclopedia but rely on the Internet for more current resources. The CREW manual provides extensive recommendations for the reference collection.

Nonprint media—CDs, DVDs, Blu-Ray, and Playaways—are evaluated using the same criteria as the print collections with the emphasis on condition, as those materials frequently have a shorter "shelf life" than books.

Adhering to the CREW standards is a good rule, although there are times when shelf space is so tight that it forces decisions one would prefer not to make, such as removing a title that appears in the Core Collection series—particularly if that item has not been popular and the author hasn't written anything else. In some cases it is necessary to eliminate entire authors who are no longer popular and whose books haven't circulated in years—even if they are listed in a standard source. In the library world there is sometimes a conflict between what "should" happen and what actually has to happen due to space constraints. These are never easy decisions, but ultimately what is best for the library must be considered.

There are certain things that libraries *do not* deselect:

- Local history or local interest materials
- Rare items
- Material that is out of print and may be irreplaceable
- Material of research value—most likely in an academic library

Disposition of Deselected Items

Once again there is a process for the deselection of materials. For each item removed:

- Insert a weeding slip and mark it with the decision
- Remove the shelf list card (or remove the record from the database)
- If other copies remain, note which copy was removed
- Remove the record from the catalog/database
- Subtract from inventory (for statistical reasons)
- Stamp "Withdrawn" or "Discard"
- Dispose of according to your policy

The disposal of withdrawn library materials can be a sensitive issue. Taxpayers don't want to see "their" library books being thrown out. Many an editorial in local newspapers has been written in indignation when someone sees that the library has done so. Nicholson Baker, noted author and essayist, sued the San Francisco Public Library in the late 1980s–early 1990s over what he claimed was irrespon-

TEXTBOX 6.4 SAMPLE WEEDING/DISPOSAL SLIP

Disposal Slip
Book Title or Call Number: _____

_____ Bindery   _____ Discard
_____ Mend/Preserve   _____ Book Sale
_____ Promote   _____ Replacement/New Edition

_____ Donate to: _____
_____ Sent to: _____
_____ Check Database for other locations of this title:
Other locations of this title: _____
Title to replace this volume: _____
Authorizing Agent: _____

sible weeding of close to 200,000 books, due to lack of space. There was more to his suit concerning other library practices, but the discovery of the dumped books was the catalyst. "'Weeding' takes place in all libraries in moderation, but the San Francisco librarians had to do it in a sweeping, indiscriminate fashion."[7] In this case there were extenuating circumstances that bolstered his case, but this just serves to illustrate the attitude and feelings of citizens when they find that their library has discarded books.

"Dumping" books is a last resort when deselecting from a collection. Other options include:

- Sell it.
  - Friends-of-the-Library groups and/or library staff routinely run book sales as fund-raisers. This can be quite profitable.
  - Library "bookstores" exist within a library, or at a remote location, have regular hours, and are staffed.
  - Local used-book stores are often looking for extra stock.
  - Online sales through eBay or Amazon, among others, can create income.
  - For-profit companies, such as Better World Books, will put a book collection bin in a convenient location and pay the library a small amount after they retrieve and resell the books.
- Donate it.
  - Nursing homes are frequently grateful for withdrawn library books, particularly if they are in large type. Prisons are also a good resource, although they may be picky about what genres and titles they will take. Hospitals and charitable groups may also be interested.
  - Daycare centers often appreciate the donation of weeded children's materials.
- Recycle it.
  - Check with your town or city sanitation department for their regulations about taking books in with regular recycling.
  - Check for a commercial recycler in your area.

- Destroy it.
  - Incinerate, if that is an option.
  - Use a Dumpster or trash bin.
  - Try to do so in a way that does not make your ownership obvious to minimize the ire of the Nicholson Bakers in your neighborhood.

There are a couple of other options for books that may be in poor condition but meet the other criteria for retention, and these include repair or rebinding as seen on the disposal slip. In general the time and expense needed to do this may outweigh the importance or value of the book. Quick and dirty repairs are a short-term solution to extend the life of a popular book; rebinding can be costly but is also an option for a book that is too important to discard. These methods will be discussed in a subsequent chapter.

If a discard is old or rare it may be potentially valuable. The value of most books is intrinsic—that is, it has value to the owner. Library markings, book jackets (or the lack thereof), and the condition of the book make a difference. Check with local experts if there are any in your area. Otherwise, try online booksellers such as ABE books, Bibliofind, Amazon, eBay, Alibris, Book Finder, and Rarebooks. You may find a number of copies of your title in various conditions and at various prices—many unsold after weeks or months on the market—but you could also hit the jackpot and find that your copy is desired at a good price.

DESELECTION OF ELECTRONIC ITEMS

E-books and databases, while not taking up physical space on a shelf, must also be considered for deselection using the same standards as print materials. Use the guidelines for retention based on use, accuracy of information, and relevance to the collection.

Electronic materials are part of the entire library collection, and a particular author or subject may be represented across several platforms. The market is expanding from popular fiction and nonfiction, and e-books are now including cookbooks and how-to or DYI titles, for example. They should be integrated and visible in the ILS. E-books that are accessed on vendor platforms (i.e., Overdrive, Axis 360) cannot be arbitrarily deselected by the subscribing library. E-books licensed for a metered number of loans partially solve that problem. Circulation, report, and collection maintenance tools provided by the platform can help the LSS evaluate the use and popularity of e-book titles.

Databases fall under the category of electronic resources. Purchased individually they can become costly to the library. Libraries participating in consortial agreements can share the cost of databases among several libraries or an entire state. One problem with this model is that not all libraries will use all of the databases, so a library may be paying for content that is underused. Individual databases also report statistics differently (by hit or by completed search, for example) making it hard to know just what content is being used by any particular library. Methods to evaluate electronic materials are improving. Since database subscriptions usually run on an annual basis, choosing alternatives allows for more frequent deselection in this area.[8]

CHAPTER SUMMARY

Inventory and deselection are integral parts of collection maintenance. Libraries can't be in the business of warehousing materials, and few libraries have the luxury of unlimited shelving. Therefore, items must be withdrawn from the collection to make room for new items as well as to maintain the integrity of the collection. Materials need to be inventoried to be sure that what is on the shelf is what is also in the library's master file, or shelf list. This is done by physically handling each item to examine for such things as age, physical condition, circulation history, and so on. Deselection, or weeding, then creates a collection that saves space and time, is more visually appealing, increases circulation, enhances the collection's reputation, and provides information on collection strengths and weaknesses. Electronic resources follow the same guidelines for retention based on use, accuracy of information, and relevance to the collection. Finally, the options for disposing of discarded materials are examined.

DISCUSSION QUESTIONS

1. What is the process of collection inventory, and what are its benefits?
2. Why do libraries deselect materials and what purpose does it serve?
3. Describe what CREW is and its importance to the library.
4. Once materials are discarded from the library collection, name some options for disposing of them.
5. Explain why electronic resources would be inventoried and weeded, since they don't take up any space in the library.

ACTIVITIES

1. Prepare a bibliography of five articles with brief notations on the principles of inventory and deselection of library resources. Your notations should be both descriptive and evaluative. Write a one-page essay about one of the trends that libraries face in this work.
2. Schedule an interview with a librarian who performs inventory and deselection, and if possible, observe his/her work. At the conclusion, summarize what you consider are the five most important principles associated with this work.

NOTES

1. "Why We Weed," Awful Library Books, last modified 2013, accessed January 26, 2016, http://awfullibrarybooks.net/why-weed/.

2. Will Manley, "The Manley Arts," *Booklist*, March 1, 1996, 1108.

3. Mary Merrill, "Weeding the Public Library Collection" (lecture, Workshop, Connecticut State Library, CT, July 12, 1990).

4. Jeannette Larson, *CREW: A Weeding Manual for Modern Libraries*, rev. ed. (Austin, TX: Texas State Library and Archives Commission, 2012).

5. Ibid., 59.

6. "Why We Weed."

7. Nicholson Baker, "The Author vs. the Library," *New Yorker*, October 26, 1996, 50.

8. Alene E. Moroni, "Weeding in a Digital Age," *Library Journal* 137, no. 15 (September 15, 2012): 26–28, accessed January 22, 2016, http://search.ebscohost.com/login.aspx?direct=true&db=tfh&AN=80445399&authtype=cookie,cpid&custid=s1024272&site=eds-live.

REFERENCES, SUGGESTED READINGS, AND WEBSITES

Awful Library Books. "Why We Weed." Awful Library Books. Last modified 2013. Accessed January 26, 2016. http://awfullibrarybooks.net/why-weed/.

Baker, Nicholson. "The Author vs. the Library." *New Yorker*, October 26, 1996, 50.

Larson, Jeannette. *CREW: A Weeding Manual for Modern Libraries*. Rev. ed. Austin, TX: Texas State Library and Archives Commission, 2012.

"Library Weeding." Video file, 2:21. YouTube. Posted by Sarala Nair, February 26, 2014. Accessed January 29, 2016. https://www.youtube.com/watch?v=3TM3YRepbPM.

Manley, Will. "The Manley Arts." *Booklist*, March 1, 1996, 1108.

Merrill, Mary. "Weeding the Public Library Collection." Lecture, Workshop, Connecticut State Library, CT, July 12, 1990.

Moroni, Alene E. "Weeding in a Digital Age." *Library Journal* 137, no. 15 (September 15, 2012): 26–28. Accessed January 22, 2016. http://search.ebscohost.com/login.aspx?direct=true&db=tfh&AN=80445399&authtype=cookie,cpid&custid=s1024272&site=eds-live.

"Weeding Your School Library." Video file, 8:53. YouTube. Posted by National Library of NZ, March 30, 2014. Accessed January 29, 2016. https://www.youtube.com/watch?v=ogUdxI-fltqg.

PART II

Tools and Technology

CHAPTER 7

Technology Tools and Services

Library Support Staff know how to use integrated library systems, other appropriate online tools, and data to manage collections, and understand the value of resource sharing agreements and apply them to collection decisions. (ALA-LSSC Competency #1 and Competency #6)

Topics Covered in This Chapter:

- A Brief Background
- Integrated Library Systems
  - Modules
- Databases
  - Expanding Resources to Which Patrons Have Access
- Networks
  - Cooperative Systems Linking Libraries
- Discovery Systems
- Other Technology Tools

Key Terms:

Barcodes: Barcodes are a machine-readable code in the form of numbers and a pattern of parallel lines of varying width. The first six numbers of the barcode are the publisher's country and identification number; the next five digits represent the book's number. The last number is called a check digit, which enables the scanner to determine if the barcode was scanned correctly. They are used in libraries to identify items and patrons.

Databases: A database is basically an electronic index or catalog. It contains an organized collection of information that allows users to search for a particular topic, article, or book. One that we are most familiar with is the library's OPAC, which is itself a database that allows users to search for resources in a library.

Discovery systems: Discovery systems, also called Web-scale discovery, means using an interface directed toward the library users to find materials in its collections, and subsequently to gain access to items of interest through the appropriate mechanisms. Discovery products tend to be independent from the specific applications that libraries use to manage resources, such as an ILS or electronic resources management systems.

Integrated Library Systems: An Integrated Library System, or ILS, is a computer system and programs that link library operations.[1] It consists of components, or modules, that do different tasks. These modules are for acquisitions, cataloging, serials, and circulating materials.

Networks: A network is a "method for sharing applications or information between two or more workstations" for the purpose of sharing information.[2] It may be as small as two computers networked to share one printer, and as large as libraries networked to form a consortium. In a typical library there may be several workstations connected to each other in one building.

Open-source software: Open-source software (OSS) allows libraries to get licensed use of the source code to modify or manipulate their ILS to suit their individual library needs. OSS is usually created by a collaborative group of individuals who then distribute the source code to programmers, who can alter it as needed.

Proprietary software: Proprietary software consists of computer programs that are the exclusive property of their developers or publishers and cannot be copied or distributed without complying with their licensing agreements. Many integrated library systems use proprietary software.[3]

Resource sharing: Resource sharing means that libraries collaborate with one another to maximize access by sharing their collections. This is done through interlibrary loan, integrated library systems, and shared databases.

A BRIEF BACKGROUND

Libraries have played an essential role in containing, sharing, and preserving information. Over time civilizations have produced and relied on various types of information, from oral stories to herd counts to tax rolls. The information explosion we have seen in the past several decades is just the most recent dilemma: How do societies maintain this collection of information? The library has evolved as the mechanism for accomplishing this purpose.

Those born in the last thirty years or so have grown up with digital technology. It's what they know and use to find information and to communicate with others. It may be a surprise to them that it wasn't always that way. The invention of writing, and media to write on, was the prevailing "technology" for a very long time. Subsequently the invention of paper, the printing press, and books changed the way society codified knowledge. Libraries became the place where books and information lived.

The first "modern" libraries, as we know them today, used classification systems to organize knowledge. We are all familiar with the Dewey Decimal System and the Library of Congress methods of cataloging and classifying books, which are still in use today. But to find those books necessitated the invention of some kind of system for finding them. Thus was born the catalog. A catalog enables a patron to look up a title, author, or subject. The very first catalogs were book catalogs. As books were added to the collection, or accessioned, they were added to the catalog by hand. If a book was withdrawn, it was crossed out. It was a cumbersome method. But then came catalog cards, 3x5 manila cards originally written by hand, then eventually typed, that were filed in alphabetical order in drawers in a cabinet called the card catalog. A patron could simply leaf through the cards in the drawer to find what they needed. When new books were added, cards were added. When books were withdrawn, their cards were pulled out of the catalog. What a great method that was! Until, of course, the invention of the computer. All bibliographic information was entered into a computer program, and patrons could use a keyboard and screen to find their books.

For computers to "read" a bibliographic record, then, meant creating codes that the computer could use to interpret the information. These were Machine Readable Computer records, or MARC records. Now online searching made it possible to find a book, rather than thumbing through drawers full of cards. In the early days, each library had its computer loaded with the information from its catalog. Computers became more sophisticated, and instead of just locating a book, the library could now check them out to individual patrons and back in again when they were returned. This could be done in a single library, and it was called a closed system.

With the Internet came the ability for libraries to electronically link their computer catalogs to one another, allowing libraries to share information and for patrons to see what books other libraries might have. "In the library world, **resource sharing** means that you are collaborating with one or more libraries to maximize access to a larger array of resources by sharing the collections of the cooperating libraries."[4] This was the beginning of the Integrated Library System.

INTEGRATED LIBRARY SYSTEMS

Modules

The **integrated library system**, or ILS, is a computer system and programs that link library operations. It consists of components, or **modules**, that do different tasks. These modules are for acquisitions, cataloging, circulation, and serials, as well as patron access:

- The acquisitions module allows for the electronic ordering and tracking of materials—books, media, e-books, and serials (although serials can have their own module). It can track funds—how much was spent—based on cost centers created in this module.
- The cataloging module is used to add and modify MARC records.
- The circulation module handles routine operations of circulation; it also tracks overdue materials, assesses fines, provides for statistics and reports relevant to the library, and keeps a database of patrons and materials.

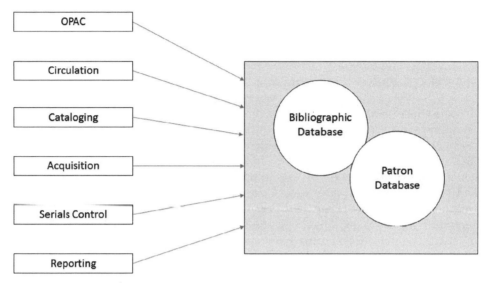

Figure 7.1. ILS module functions. *Courtesy of the author*

- The serials module keeps track of journals, newspapers, and other items that come on a regular schedule. It can also track funds expended.
- The online public catalog, or OPAC, allows for the searching of the collection.

Benefits of an ILS

An ILS provides many benefits such as keyword searching of a variety of fields, providing a more complete view of collection content. Additionally,

- it reduces staff time committed to repetitive and less challenging tasks;
- it reduces the amount of time spent walking from the desk to paper-based files;
- it increases productivity;
- it increases accuracy;
- it increases the speed of checkout and online ordering;
- it provides for files shared at the desktop level, and therefore
- it can provide the advantage of a library-wide, unified database
  - such as an OPAC (online public access computer),
  - a LAN (computers networked within a building),
  - a WAN (computers linked to others outside the building, in remote locations);
- it can provide for statistics;
- the OPAC allows remote access 24/7.

Ultimately it provides end users with greater access to information.

These systems are integrated, so they can be accessed from a single point. There are two graphical interfaces, or two ways to access: staff access and patron access. Patrons can only see what's in the catalog; they cannot modify it. But by logging in to their own account, a patron may change their password and request and renew materials. Staff access allows librarians to use some or all of the modules to catalog, order materials, set permissions, run reports, or change circulation parameters, among other things.

The ILS uses a barcode scanner in the circulation interface both to identify the patron and the item being borrowed. The scanner—handheld or mounted—is programmed to recognize the **barcode** symbology of both patrons and items. A computer can be set to make a sound, like a beep or chime, when a barcode is scanned. The scanner will appear to work whether you scan a book or a can of peas. It is important, therefore, for LSS to understand that just because the chime sounds does not mean the information has been accepted—it has to be able to interpret the programmed barcode. Reading the screen is a habit LSS should quickly adopt to be sure the information did indeed register into the program. It ensures that the right information has been accepted.

There are a multitude of integrated library systems on the market, and it's important for LSS to know which one they use, what their network consists of, what the limitations of the network are, and how to troubleshoot when the system is not working.

Circulation systems may be integrated (e.g., it may have modules for circulation, online catalog, and acquisitions); or stand-alone (a single module or several modules that do not share data, or one that is not connected to a network of libraries). These modules work together to "share" data; this is a multifunction system set up by the vendor.[5] The annual "Library Systems Report" by Marshall Breeding, an independent library consultant, includes the vendor profiles of several dozen companies that produce automated library systems.[6] These company-owned products are proprietary and changes can only be made by the vendor. The annual costs of these systems can be many thousands of dollars for support, maintenance, and upgrades.[7] Some familiar examples of these products include Verso from Autographics, Sirsi/Dynix Symphony from Sirsi/Dynix, Destiny by Follet, and Millenium by Innovative Interfaces.

Some libraries may keep their systems for ten years, some up to twenty-five years without changing. Libraries need to keep up to date on ILS for the newest technology and best value for their library. However, we need to ask ourselves if we are providing the services that are appropriate for patrons and staff before changing systems—in other words, make sure you know what works best for staff and patrons. Don't embrace customization as much as learning what is there and how to use it. If everything is working well, there may be no need to change.[8]

If the need to change systems does occur, instead of buying proprietary software products such as those mentioned above, a library can choose open-source software (OSS). In another article by Breeding, "Open Source Library Automation," he describes the open-source model as "free to use, free to modify, and free to share."[9] With open-source software, libraries get licensed use of the source code and can modify or manipulate their ILS to suit their individual library needs. OSS is usually created by a collaborative group of individuals who then distribute the source code to programmers, who can alter it as needed. OSS allows for faster improvements to the software than a vendor-owned system.[10] Systems using open-source software function the same way as any ILS; the difference is transparent to the user. Probably the most familiar names in open-source software are Koha, by LibLime, and

Evergreen ILS, by Evergreen. Several sources agree that there are several reasons that open-source software is preferable to proprietary software.[11] Among them are:

1. Security
2. Quality
3. Better-quality code
4. Customizability
5. Freedom
6. Flexibility
7. Interoperability
8. Rapid innovation
9. Auditability
10. Support options
11. Cost

Other trends that may be possible in future iterations of the ILS include simply scanning a patron's driver's license to automatically create his library account or providing real-time integrated downloads of ordered materials from vendors. Additionally, cloud developments may allow libraries to collaborate across different systems, within and across states.[12]

Which system a library uses depends on the size of the collection, the volume of activity, and the cost both to buy in and to maintain on an annual basis. When my library first automated, we chose a stand-alone system designed for small libraries, and pricing was based on the size of the collection. It did everything we needed it to do, but it was a closed system—that is, it only operated in-house, not on the Web. We were not able to connect remotely or see the catalogs of any other libraries. We subsequently joined a consortium of several libraries, and while it was a bit more cumbersome, the ability to share catalogs more than made up for it. While individual integrated library systems may vary from library to library, they *all* share several characteristics. They should all

1. Be relatively easy to use
2. Be reliable
3. Identify materials borrowed and their due date
4. Provide a record of overdue materials
5. Provide for holds or reserves of requested materials
6. Automatically delete the link between user and item
7. Allow for the creation of statistics
8. Be cost effective
9. Integrate with other modules in the ILS

The use of current technology allows the LSS to search and choose other resources as well to satisfy patron needs beyond the ILS. The Internet and Web technology have had a substantial impact on library activities. Libraries have gone beyond simply linking their systems to other systems, and now offer online services such as RSS feeds, blogs, and all manner of social media—which seem to spring up virtually overnight. Twitter, Snapchat, Instagram, Facebook, YouTube, Tumblr, Flicker, Pinterest, Linked In, and Google+ allow LSS to use these technologies to communicate with patrons about what new material or events may be going on at the library.

DATABASES

A **database** is basically an electronic index or catalog. It contains an organized collection of information that allows users to search for a particular topic, article, or book. One that we are most familiar with is the library's OPAC, which is a database that allows users to search for resources in one library. A library may also be part of a consortium of several libraries, meaning that their catalogs are linked. Searching one OPAC can reveal resources that other libraries own.

But libraries are not just about books. In yet another way to expand resources to which patrons have access, a library's OPAC may provide electronic databases to which the library would subscribe. These databases offer a wide variety of published materials, including full-text articles from journals and other serials that are also searchable by keyword, author, title, or subject. With the number of databases available, and usually limited funds, a library has to carefully decide what databases they are going to subscribe to, as fees can range in the thousands of dollars for just one year. We learned in chapter 3 about how to choose books and media by using review sources. Many of these same sources can be helpful in reviewing databases.

Databases, however, are the most expensive investment of all of the library's nonprint resources. "Access to databases may be leased on an individual basis by the library, received as part of state grants or funding, or arranged through a consortial agreement"[13] (shared by several libraries). In an academic library, databases can take up to 75 to 80 percent of the library budget, while print monographs may only be about 25 percent. Criteria used to determine the library's choice of database may include a number of factors, including the size of the library, the reliability and reputation of the database, and ultimately the cost. Most commercial databases come "bundled" or packaged with a predetermined number of sources included for library or institutional access. Additionally the reputation of the journals, the depth of content, currency or updating of the database, ease of use and user friendliness are important factors when subscribing to a database.[14]

Additional factors include technical feasibility such as availability and compatibility of the e-resources with existing hardware, vendor support, and currency of the information. As some electronic resources lag behind the print version, it's important that the LSS be aware of this—as users may assume they are getting the most current information.

Expanding Resources to Which Patrons Have Access

A database may include more resources than your library needs, however, so a library may be paying for those that will go unused. Other database providers may charge the library on a per-use basis: this means that there is a charge for every search conducted in the library whether it was completed or not. Still others charge on the basis of population or student body figures, most common in academic libraries. Some popular databases available to public, school, and academic libraries include Gale Virtual Reference Library, Zinio for Libraries, Proquest, EBSCO, Gale Cengage, and Questia.[15] These sources provide content that includes full-text journals, magazines, reports, essays, and more, and they are widely available through libraries. Other options for school and public libraries include Tumblebooks and ScholasticFlix, and all libraries can choose the eBook and eContent provider BiblioBoard. The LSS must become familiar with the resources available in their own library's electronic collection.

Currently Connecticut uses an EBSCO database provided by the state library, called ResearchIT CT. Some of the resources that LSS can use to help patrons find information include Academic Search Premier, Masterfile, Eric, Heritage Quest and Ancestry, Biography Reference Center, Referencia Latina, and several targeted for those in elementary school to college. This is a comprehensive selection. When I was working, it cost the library $300 a year to subscribe—which I thought was a bargain! Another example of a state-sponsored database that LSS can point users to is Pennsylvania's Power Library, an electronic database that gives 24/7 access to dozens of resources including newspapers, magazines, journals, historical documents and photos, online databases, and e-books.

Speaking of bargains, there are a number of free databases that the LSS should be aware of. The Library of Congress offers *E-Resources Online Catalog*; the New York Public Library offers *Public Domain Collections: Free to Share & Reuse; AP Images* is a free source for editorial and creative photos and images, and *Open Access Journals* offered by Elsevier offers peer-reviewed material in the sciences.

But, you may wonder, what about the Internet? Patrons are most likely to go immediately to Google, Bing, and other search engines. LSS must know that they do not necessarily provide the most accurate information. The postings are not

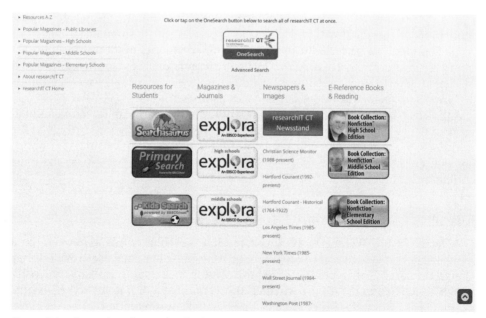

Figure 7.2. Screenshot of researchIT database. *researchIT CT State Library*

reviewed and can contain incorrect information. Wikipedia, in particular, can be notoriously misleading, as the content is user contributed without oversight. Just because it's on the Web doesn't mean it's correct! LSS should steer patrons to the subscription databases, as it assures timely and accurate information.

NETWORKS

A **network** is a "method for sharing applications or information between two or more workstations."[16] It may be as small as two computers networked to share one printer, and as large as libraries networked to form a consortium. In a typical library there may be several workstations connected to each other in one building. This is called a LAN, or Local Area Network. A WAN, or Wide Area Network, exists over a large geographic area and connects smaller networks, including LANS. It is "similar

Figure 7.3. Computer network

to a banking system, where hundreds of branches in different cities are connected with each other in order to share their official data."[17] Once done only by using extensive cabling, now they are often wireless. So it goes with library networks.

COOPERATIVE SYSTEMS LINKING LIBRARIES

A cooperative is basically a group working together willingly for the common good. When libraries share electronic resources or databases, it creates a cooperative. There are several kinds that apply to libraries:

- Local library networks working together to form a consortium of integrated library systems (ILS) is a cooperative.
- Larger cooperative networks include, for example, individual state libraries, which provide a database of the holdings of all participating individual libraries in the state, including public, school, special, and academic. It allows for the searching of materials anywhere in the state for the purpose of interlibrary loans (ILL).
- An example of a regional network is Lyrasis, a membership cooperative of libraries combining the former NELINET (New England), SOLINET (the Atlanta area), and PALINET (the mid-Atlantic region).[18]
- Nationally and globally the major cooperative network is OCLC, a nonprofit, membership-based computer library service dedicated to furthering access to the world's information.

The size and cost make these last two networks more appropriate for academic and large public library systems. It is an expensive way to provide ILL, as fees to join range from several hundreds of dollars for a regional consortium to many thousands of dollars for systems such as OCLC.

DISCOVERY SYSTEMS

Traditional library information systems, such as library catalogs and databases, are referred to as search systems. The way we are used to searching is by entering a term into the search box and finding information contained in the index of that database. Using a **discovery system**, also called Web-scale discovery, means using an interface directed toward the library users to find materials in its collections, and subsequently to gain access to items of interest through other mechanisms. Discovery products tend to be independent from the specific applications that libraries use to manage resources, such as an ILS or electronic resources management systems. Discovery systems usually provide relevancy-based ordering of search results with the ability to narrow results according to specific categories to identify related materials or to refine search queries.[19]

According to a presentation given by Tamar Sadeh of Ex Libris Group, Jerusalem, Israel, at a conference of the IFLA (International Federation of Library Associations) in 2013,

In recent years, library users have shifted from searching in library catalogs and scholarly databases to searching in library discovery systems. This shift has introduced a fundamental change in the information-seeking process. Discovery systems provide access to a large, diverse information landscape of scholarly materials—regardless of where the materials are located, what format they are in, and whether the library owns them or subscribes to them. At the same time, these systems typically offer simple, Google-like searching as the default option, to accommodate the expectations of today's users. With this type of searching, users do not spend much time formulating queries, and their queries often yield large result sets; therefore, discovery systems focus on relevance ranking and on tools that help users easily navigate and refine result sets.[20]

Common features of discovery layers for Web-scale discovery services include the following:

- Single search across the central index
- Fast response time
- Relevancy-ranked results list
- Facets, sort, and other tools for refining and using the results
- Connections to full text via direct links and OpenURL
- End-user accounts and features[21]

A discovery system uses a preselected central index gathered from multiple sources: the central index is content, and the discovery layer is the interface. The difference, then, between a regular search and a search using a discovery system is that the results are "tailored" to your request by searching a multitude of local, remote, and open-access content not limited to your own library's database. This comes with a price—it is only offered through four vendors: EBSCO's Discovery Service (EDS), Ex Libris's Primo Central Index (PCI), Serials Solutions' Summon (SSS), and OCLC's WorldCat Local (WCL).[22]

OTHER TECHNOLOGY TOOLS

No assessment of technology tools is complete without acknowledging the personal devices that patrons use. LSS should be very familiar with how to assist users in downloading e-books—from several platforms—to digital readers including all manner of Kindles, Nooks, Sony Readers (Touch and Pocket), Kobo, iPhones, Droids—and whatever new technology comes down the pike by the next time you blink.

Laptops are no longer the latest thing, but a variety of notebooks, tablets, iPads, and similar devices have made their way into your library, and LSS may expect to be asked to help with using them for accessing library catalogs and databases, and downloading anything from e-books to music to streaming video from the library's own catalog, a service such as Overdrive or Axis 360, or from a commercial vendor like Amazon.

"Web and mobile technologies are offering libraries a new world of opportunities to engage patrons. Ultra-popular social media websites and apps combined with the availability of affordable cloud-based services and the evolution and adoption of mobile devices are enabling librarians to share and build communities, store and analyze large collections of data, create digital collections, and access information and services in ways never thought about before."[23]

As libraries provide more and more digital resources, storage may become a problem. Using cloud technology allows for secure storage and easy access and adds the option of providing a cloud-based collection. Libraries are increasingly offering mobile websites, screencasts, Google Voice for text reference, and personas (fictional depictions of a library's target audience).[24] LSS can and should play an important part in implementing these technologies. If you can imagine it, it will be coming soon to a library near you.

CHAPTER SUMMARY

In this chapter we discussed trends in library technology from integrated library systems to the latest in mobile applications. Technology tools exist both to provide content and service to the patron and to help LSS enable these services. Electronic databases can be linked to cooperatively share resources locally and globally. The use of discovery systems will ultimately redefine the way we search, offering quicker and more targeted results.

DISCUSSION QUESTIONS

1. What are some of the benefits of using an integrated library system (ILS)?
2. Describe the difference between proprietary and open-source software for libraries.
3. Explain what functions the various modules in an ILS perform.
4. Describe a library partnership in your state or region.
5. What is a cooperative and how does it pertain to libraries?

ACTIVITIES

1. Research three different ILS systems and describe the features they offer in the area of collection management. Based on your analysis, what functions would you choose from each system, and why?
2. Explain how you would answer a user who says, "I don't want my library's materials to be shared with other libraries. I want them to stay right here because my tax dollars paid for them!"

NOTES

1. G. Edward Evans, Sheila S. Intner, and Jean Weihs, *Introduction to Technical Services*, 8th ed., Library and Information Science Text Series (Santa Barbara, CA: Libraries Unlimited, 2011), 60.

2. John J. Burke, *Library Technology Companion*, 4th ed. (Chicago, IL: Neal-Schuman, 2013), 224.

3. "Proprietary software," *Business Dictionary*, accessed February 11, 2016, http://www.businessdictionary.com/definition/proprietary-software.html.

4. Annette Lamb, "Acquisitions and Management of Knowledge and Information," *Eduscapes*, last modified 2015, accessed March 12, 2016, http://eduscapes.com/collection/12.htm.

5. J. Burke, *Library Technology Companion*, 2nd ed. (New York, NY: Neal-Schuman, 2006), 75.

6. Marshall Breeding, "Library Systems Report," *American Libraries*, last modified May 1, 2015, accessed February 5, 2016, http://americanlibrariesmagazine.org/2015/05/01/library-systems-report.

7. Hali R. Keeler, *Foundations of Library Service*, Library Support Staff Handbooks 1 (Lanham, MD: Rowman & Littlefield, 2015), 3.

8. "American Libraries Live: Integrated Library Systems," video file, YouTube, posted by Dan Freeman, May 2015, accessed February 6, 2016, https://www.youtube.com/watch?v=F8X-gyROqOm0.

9. Marshall Breeding, "Open Source Library Automation: Overview and Perspective," *Library Technology Reports*, accessed February 6, 2016, https://www.webjunction.org/content/dam/WebJunction/Documents/webJunction/LTR_44n8_nov08_chap1.pdf.

10. Burke, *Library Technology Companion*, 85.

11. Katherine Noyes, "10 Reasons Open Source Is Good for Business," *PCWorld*, November 5, 2010, accessed February 9, 2016, http://www.pcworld.com/article/209891/10_reasons_open_source_is_good_for_business.html; Vala Afshar, "10 Reasons to Use Open Source Software Defined Networking," *Huffington Post*, last modified September 4, 2014, accessed February 9, 2016, http://www.huffingtonpost.com/vala-afshar/10-reasons-to-use-open-so_b_5766718.html.

12. "Integrated Library Systems," video file.

13. Ibid.

14. Marie Keen Shaw, *Library Technology and Digital Resources: An Introduction for Support Staff*, Library Support Staff Handbooks (Lanham, MD: Rowman and Littlefield, 2015), 86.

15. Henrietta Thornton-Verma, "Databases: What You're Loving, What's Upcoming," last modified November 1, 2013, accessed December 19, 2015, http://search.ebscohost.com/login.aspx?direct=true&db=aph&AN=83527001&authtype=cookie,cpid&custid=s1024272&site=e-host-live&scope=site.

16. Burke, *Library Technology Companion*, 224.

17. "Wide Area Network (WAN)," *Techopedia*, last modified 2016, accessed February 10, 2016, https://www.techopedia.com/definition/5409/wide-area-network-wan.

18. Marshall Breeding, "SOLINET, PALINET and NELINET Merge to Form Lyrasis," *Smart Libraries Newsletter* 29, no. 7 (March 1, 2010), 2–3, accessed February 25, 2015, http://www.librarytechnology.org/ltg-displaytext.pl?RC=14582.

19. "Library Technology Guides," Library Technology, last modified 2010, accessed February 11, 2016, http://www.librarytechnology.org/discovery/.

20. Tamar Sadeh, "From Search to Discovery" (lecture, IFLA World Information and Library Congress, June 19, 2013).

21. Athena Hoeppner, "The Ins and Outs of Evaluating Web-Scale Discovery Services," *Information Today*, last modified April 11, 2012, accessed February 11, 2016, http://www.infotoday.com/cilmag/apr12/Hoeppner-Web-Scale-Discovery-Services.shtml.

22. Ibid.

23. Ellyssa Kroski, "10 Great Technology Initiatives for Your Library," American Libraries, last modified February 26, 2013, accessed February 11, 2016, http://americanlibrariesmagazine.org/2013/02/27/10-great-technology-initiatives-for-your-library/.

24. Ibid.

REFERENCES, SUGGESTED READINGS, AND WEBSITES

Afshar, Vala. "10 Reasons to Use Open Source Software Defined Networking." *Huffington Post.* Last modified September 4, 2014. Accessed February 9, 2016. http://www.huffingtonpost. com/vala-afshar/10-reasons-to-use-open-so_b_5766718.html.

"American Libraries Live: Integrated Library Systems." Video file. YouTube. Posted by Dan Freeman, May 2015. Accessed February 6, 2016. https://www.youtube.com/watch?v=F8X-gyROqOm0.

Breeding, Marshall. "Library Systems Report." *American Libraries.* Last modified May 1, 2015. Accessed February 5, 2016. http://americanlibrariesmagazine.org/2015/05/01/library-systems-report/.

———. "Library Technology Guides." *Library Technology.* Last modified 2010. Accessed February 11, 2016. http://www.librarytechnology.org/discovery/.

———. "A Look at Tech Patron Engaging Products in the Exhibit Hall." *American Libraries.* Last modified July 23, 2015. Accessed February 9, 2016. http://americanlibrariesmagazine. org/2015/07/23/a-look-at-tech/.

———. "Open Source Library Automation: Overview and Perspective." *Library Technology Reports.* Accessed February 6, 2016. https://www.webjunction.org/content/dam/WebJunction/ Documents/webJunction/LTR_44n8_nov08_chap1.pdf.

Burke, John J. *Library Technology Companion.* 2nd ed. New York, NY: Neal-Schuman, 2006.

Encyclopaedia Britannica. "The PC Revolution." *Encyclopaedia Britannica Online.* Last modified November 2010. Accessed February 4, 2016. http://newsletters.britannica.com/newsletter_NOV10.html.

Evans, G. Edward, Sheila S. Intner, and Jean Weihs. *Introduction to Technical Services.* 8th ed. Library and Information Science Text Series. Santa Barbara, CA: Libraries Unlimited, 2011.

Hoeppner, Athena. "The Ins and Outs of Evaluating Web-Scale Discovery Services." *Information Today.* Last modified April 11, 2012. Accessed February 11, 2016. http://www.infotoday. com/cilmag/apr12/Hoeppner-Web-Scale-Discovery-Services.shtml.

Keeler, Hali R. *Foundations of Library Service.* Library Support Staff Handbooks 1. Lanham, MD: Rowman & Littlefield, 2015.

Kroski, Ellyssa. "10 Great Technology Initiatives for Your Library." *American Libraries.* Last modified February 26, 2013. Accessed February 11, 2016. http://americanlibrariesmagazine. org/2013/02/27/10-great-technology-initiatives-for-your-library/.

Miller, Rebecca K., Caroline Meier, and Heather Moorefield-Lang. "Dispatches from the Field: The Tao of Tablets." *American Libraries* 44, nos. 3/4 (March/April 2013): 20.

Noyes, Katherine. "10 Reasons Open Source Is Good for Business." *PCWorld*, November 5, 2010. Accessed February 9, 2016. http://www.pcworld.com/article/209891/10_reasons_ open_source_is_good_for_business.html.

Sadeh, Tamar. "From Search to Discovery" (lecture, IFLA World Information and Library Congress, June 19, 2013).

Sharon, Johnson, Ole Gunnar Evensen, Julia Gelfand, Glenda Lammera, Lynn Sipe, and Nadia Zilper. "Key Issues for E-Resource Collection Development: A Guide for Libraries." The International Federation of Library Associations and Institutions. Last modified August 2012. Accessed December 18, 2015. http://www.ifla.org/publications/key-issues-for-e-resource-collection-development-a-guide-for-libraries.

Shaw, Marie Keen. *Library Technology and Digital Resources.* Library Support Staff Handbooks 2. Lanham, MD: Rowman & Littlefield, 2015.

Techopedia. "Wide Area Network (WAN)." *Techopedia.* Last modified 2016. Accessed February 10, 2016. https://www.techopedia.com/definition/5409/wide-area-network-wan.

Thornton-Verma, Henrietta. "Databases: What You're Loving, What's Upcoming." Last modified November 1, 2013. Accessed December 19, 2015. http://search.ebscohost.com/login.aspx?direct=true&db=aph&AN=83527001&authtype=cookie,cpid&custid=s1024272&site=ehost-live&scope=site.

Webfinance, Inc. "Proprietary software." *Business Dictionary*. Accessed February 11, 2016. http://www.businessdictionary.com/definition/proprietary-software.html.

CHAPTER 8

Collection Statistics and Use

Library Support Staff know how to use integrated library systems, other appropriate online tools, and data to manage collections. (ALA-LSSC Competency #1)

Topics covered in this chapter:

- Collection Statistics
  - What Statistics Are
  - Why We Collect Statistics
  - How We Collect Statistics
- Collection Reports
  - Circulation—Print and Nonprint
  - Circulation—Electronic
- Item Reports
  - Age and Date of Items
  - Collection Strengths and Weaknesses
- Other Reports
  - Interlibrary Loan
  - Program Statistics
  - Reference Transactions
- Use of Statistical Data
  - State Library Statistical Reports
  - Library Planning
  - Budgets

Key Terms:

AENGLC rank: AENGLC rank means the adjusted equalized net grand list per capita, a measure of town wealth calculated annually. The lower the number is, the wealthier the town. This is an important factor when comparing libraries in different parts of the state. While helpful, at this time it is only used in Connecticut.

Collection reports: A collection report is run on an automated library system to provide statistical information of the items in a particular collection, such as the monthly circulation of children's books. It provides a snapshot of the activity of that area.

Integrated Library Systems: An integrated library system, or ILS, is a computer system and programs that link library operations.[1] It consists of components, or modules, that do different tasks. These modules are for acquisitions, cataloging, serials, and circulating materials.

Item reports: Item reports are those run by an automated system that are specific to a particular item or category, such as all items in a certain Dewey number, or all DVDs that the library owns. Item reports are an important part of evaluating a collection.

Programming: Programming is the offering of events, classes, lectures, etc. to the variety of library patrons in any given community. They serve to bring people to the library as well as create community spirit. Keeping statistics on library programs is valuable when evaluating library services.

Statistics: Statistics is the practice dealing with the collection, analysis, interpretation, and presentation of large quantities of numerical data. It is a useful tool for libraries to evaluate their collections and services.

In chapter 7 we addressed most of LSSC Competency 1: Integrated Library Systems, (ILS), databases, networks and other cooperative tools, and discovery systems. We did not, however, address the second part of that competency: *data to manage collections*. In this chapter we will be looking at how to use data, or statistics, to analyze the library collection for use, strengths, and weaknesses. We will see how vendors provide usage statistics for online resources. We will, in fact, see all of the ways that statistics can help a library evaluate where they are and how to plan for the future. When collected properly and presented effectively, statistics can be an invaluable tool for improving community relations, library service, and funding. LSS can use statistics as a publicity and information tool as well.

While school and academic libraries participate in statistical surveys under the aegis of the NCES (National Center for Educational Statistics), professional associations, and funding bodies, they have a slightly different focus than what is required of public libraries. For the purpose of this chapter, we will be dealing with public libraries.

COLLECTION STATISTICS

What Statistics Are

Statistics is the collection, analysis, interpretation, and presentation of large quantities of numerical data. If you will remember, one of the functions of a good

ILS is the ability to collect statistics and perform reports based on those statistics. It can be as simple as finding out how many items circulated at the end of the day. Prior to automation, LSS in some libraries kept circulation statistics on a daily basis by literally counting the cards that were taken out of the books and stamped with a due date when they were checked out. They would then be sorted (by fiction, nonfiction, children's, teens, etc.) and counted and the numbers transferred into a record book: day by day, week by week, month by month, and year after year. Albeit low-tech, this was the statistical record of the library's circulation.

Why We Collect Statistics

We collect statistics because someone wants to know something. Libraries are responsible for the regulatory demands of their funding body, as we learned in the previous chapter. They need to be able to show that they are providing worth to their funders by quantifying the information that shows, for example, the number of materials being circulated in a given time period, and the cost per capita of that circulation. Statistical reports are required for the library governing body, the cooperative or network a library may belong to, and the state.

How We Collect Statistics

This is where integrated library systems come in. An ILS comes with predetermined report functions that allow a library to track functions and operations. Statistic reports produce tables of information gathered from the system to create a statistics report type. For example, a report can be generated to list fiction books that have not circulated in the past five years. Given this information, the LSS can pull those particular books from the shelf and put them on a cart for a librarian to review. The report only tells what has not circulated in that time period; it is up to someone to decide if they will stay in the collection or be withdrawn. This will be discussed a little later on when we get into specific reports and how they are used.

Public library statistics are collected annually from over nine thousand public libraries through the Public Library Survey (PLS) and disseminated by IMLS (Institute for Museum and Library Services).[2]

COLLECTION REPORTS

Circulation: Print and Nonprint

There are numerous **collection reports** that can be generated from the ILS. Let's begin with circulation reports. While statistical reports can be run anytime one is needed, most libraries will run them monthly, as this can correlate with the requirements of reporting agencies such as the state library. In the sample circulation report in table 8.1, this library tracks all formats: print and nonprint, including books, books on CD, museum passes, and Playaway.

Table 8.1. Monthly Circulation Statistics

	Adult	**Juvenile**	**YA**	**Total**
Books	6137	6582	786	13505
Bks-on-CD	1422	76	48	1546
Feat.DVD	2471	1029	5	3505
ILL_Bk	31	0	0	31
Lang CD	21	2	4	23
Magazine	426	2	4	432
Music CD	340	92	0	432
NF-DVD	314	33	1	348
Passes	22	0	0	22
Playaway	167	50	10	227
Total	11351	7836	858	20071

Circulation reports can be further refined by item. The sample report in table 8.2 is for just Playaway circulation for one month in three categories: adult, juvenile, and YA.

Other specific circulation reports can include only nonfiction, books-on-CD, feature DVDs (as opposed to nonfiction DVDs), juvenile materials, and so on.

Circulation—Electronic

Circulation statistics for **electronic** materials are not gathered from the ILS but from the digital vendors' sites themselves. OverDrive, a widely used product that was mentioned in a previous chapter, provides a reports function. Although Over-Drive began as a provider of electronic books in several formats for download to a device, it now provides, in addition to e-books, audio content, streaming video, magazines, MP3 audiobooks, and more. A report for checkouts for a given day, week, or month can provide the information in the next table, which can be reformatted into a spreadsheet. This report will also include information on items that have been reserved or are pending. According to a user statistic survey of vendor-provided usages statistics conducted in 2010, although most tried to run reports monthly, some could only do so as needed, ongoing throughout the year, or not on any specific basis.[3]

Statistics from databases such as the one pictured in chapter 7 are also provided by the vendor. The last database I worked with was through the state library, and they would automatically generate a monthly report to show database use for each

Table 8.2. Monthly Circulation of Playaways

Adult	155
Juvenile	44
YA	8
Total	207

Table 8.3.   Sample OverDrive Circulation Report

Pending (video)	1
Adobe PDF e-Book	1
Overdrive Listen	3
Streaming Video	5
Pending (audiobook)	27
OverDrive Read	32
Pending (e-Book)	56
Adobe EPUB e-Book	92
OverDrive MP3 Audiobook	112
NOOK Periodicals	125
Kindle Book	271
Total	725

available resource. It showed how many times a resource was accessed, how many searches were initiated, and how many searches were completed. This allows for monitoring the use of the subscriptions in that database. Since it was a resource provided by the state library, and not my own purchase, it made little difference except to see what resources my patrons used. However, those statistics would be very important to the state when it came time to renew the license. If libraries all over the state reported low usage of particular resources, this could influence whether that resource would be renewed.

ITEM REPORTS

Age and Date of Items

Besides circulation reports, the ILS can provide **item reports**. As mentioned earlier in this chapter, a library wants to know about the collection—what books have not been off the shelf in five or more years, what areas of the collection are being well used, and which areas are being underused. Statistical reports can be run for just about any reason, as most offer flexibility in creating or modifying reports. They can be run to count items in a category such as by call number, item numbers, or item titles. Reports can show the average date of publication or the average price of books.

The report function of an ILS usually offers tabs at the top of the page that list the options available for reports; these tabs then open up a menu of reports from which to choose. In a large or academic library this may be done only by librarians, but in smaller libraries or departments, LSS can be tasked with running some item reports. Many of these reports are "canned"—that is, they are programmed into the ILS and may only need dates or other parameters added.

As an example, a report might be run on the 600s: technology, including medicine and health. Because of changes in these fields it is imperative that books in those areas remain current. A report can be run of all books from 600 to 699.9. This report can tell the LSS the ages of all the items in this category. It can also tell how many books there are in the collection on human anatomy, medicine and health, and pharmacology—and how often they circulate. While an older book on human anatomy is probably still useful, older books on science or medicine can be out of date—sometimes dangerously so. The dates are a red flag that those particular books should be examined. The LSS takes the book cart, finds the suspect titles, and pulls them off the shelf for further examination by the librarian. The existence of current Web sources in health and medicine may suggest that some of these older books would not be replaced, although some standard sources likely would be.

An older book is not necessarily a candidate for withdrawal. Literature, poetry, biographies of historic figures, works of philosophy or art—these items may stay on the shelf regardless of age because of their intrinsic and lasting value.

Fiction reports can similarly be run by author, or all authors beginning with *A*. This will show all items by a particular author and their publication dates, which can reveal, for example, a very prolific author who has written dozens of books but nothing in the past five to seven years and none that circulate anymore. According to the "just in case" theory, it may be appropriate to discard all of this author's books to make room for newer authors and titles. It is often difficult to make those decisions in spite of the evidence, as some staff members could remember when those authors' books flew off the shelf. There is little room for sentimentality when the statistics show inactivity, particularly with fiction authors, who may have a brief run of popularity.

Collection Strengths and Weaknesses

A good way to judge the strengths and weaknesses of a collection is to run an item report in a particular Dewey or LC area. An average date report can reflect strengths

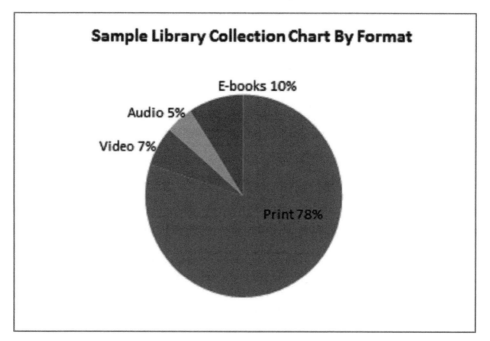

Figure 8.1.   Sample library collection charts for one fiscal year. *Groton Public Library*

and weaknesses in the collection by finding that certain categories are lacking in current materials. It may show that the 640s, cookbooks, have hundreds of titles— but that may not be a problem because in most libraries cookbooks are enormously popular. It may also show a lesser number of items in the 809 area, which is literary criticism, an area that may need fewer titles. It may also show that there are not enough cookbooks to meet the demand, or too few biographies. Libraries want and need a balanced collection, but not at the expense of holding on to little-used books. As we saw in the chapter on deselection, fewer books on a shelf make the remaining books more visible.

In determining a collection's strengths and weaknesses it is helpful to know the makeup of the collection in terms of the percentage of adult materials to children's or teen's materials; print to nonprint; feature DVDs to nonfiction DVDs. Much of this relies on the library's community assessment, or demographic makeup, as was discussed in chapter 1. A statistical report can provide that information.

OTHER REPORTS

Interlibrary Loan

No library can own everything. Interlibrary loan (ILL) is the process by which a library borrows an item from another library for one of its users. It is another method of providing access to information. The Interlibrary Loan Code for the United States that guides this practice was prepared by the Reference and User Services Association of the American Library Association.

Most state and regional systems will have their own codes that mirror that of ALA, and all LSS should be familiar with it. It occurs in virtually every library—public, academic, and in some cases, school libraries. Because ILL is regulated, so to speak, it is necessary to provide statistical information gleaned from the ILS to the state or regional system that provides the service. Statistics include how many items a library requests to borrow and how many of those requests are filled; they also include how many items a library requests to borrow for their patrons, and how many of those requests are filled. These statistics are needed so the region or state that provides the service can calculate the cost of each transaction. ILL is free for patrons, but costs are incurred both by LSS performing ILL activities (their time), the delivery system to get the items to other libraries, and the region or state that ultimately funds it.

Program Statistics

Libraries offer various programs, which can be broken down into three types: educational, recreational, and outreach.[4] We offer programming for tangible reasons: it brings people into the library. We do it for intangible reasons: to expose patrons to art, music, and the humanities. We do it, also, for the sake of community spirit and connections. Educational programs can include offering lifelong learning opportunities; recreational programs offer films, lectures, and gaming; and outreach programs can include library service to the homebound, nursing homes, or daycare centers. Whatever the activity, it is important to keep records of the kinds of pro-

---

TEXTBOX 8.1 SAMPLE ILL STATISTICS REPORTING CHART

Borrowing Requests:

Material your library requests from other libraries
Number of borrowing requests filled from other libraries _____
Number of borrowing requests filled from out-of-state libraries _____

Lending Requests:

Material your library supplies to other libraries
Number of filled lending requests supplied to other libraries
Number of filled lending requests supplied to out-of-state libraries _____

Use the totals to help fill out your ILL questions on the Annual Report/Survey

---

grams given and for which age groups. Also to be included is the number of people who attend.

Programs are extremely labor intensive, from finding a speaker or deciding on an activity to booking the program space, advertising the program, and setting up the room. Having attendance records gives LSS a base of attendees to invite, and also provides for tracking by age or other criteria. These statistics are critical to justifying the inclusion of funds for programming to the library's funding source—board, town, or county.

These statistics are not provided through an ILS but can be designed and be created in management and tracking software, or on Excel spreadsheets. Take a look at a sample program statistics report by age and attendance in table 8.4.

Reference Transactions

Reference transactions are information contacts that involve the knowledge, use, recommendations, interpretation, or instruction in the use of one or more information sources by a member of the library staff. It includes information and referral

Table 8.4.   Sample Program Attendance Statistics

Adult		Children		Teen	
Name	#	Name	#	Name	#
Book discussion	15	Story Time for Toddlers	25	Manga club	5
Film Fest	25	Story Time for Preschool	17	Teen book group	7
Coloring for grown ups	30	Saturday crafts	30	Pizza and movie	12
Intro to Computers	10	After-school book group	8	Game night	8
Kindle Fire Basics	6			After-school fun!	5
Total	86		80		37

services. It does not include directional assistance.[5] Many libraries track these trans-actions for statistical purposes as well, to measure the effectiveness of a library's reference services.

The quantity of materials added to, and withdrawn from, the collection is another statistic that libraries keep in order to track the number of items in a collection on a regular basis. The size of a collection can influence such things as subscription fees to an ILS, database, or any other service for which the cost is calculated according to the size of the collection.

USE OF STATISTICAL DATA

State Library Statistical Reports

As mentioned previously, public libraries across the country are required to pro-vide very specific information in order for the state to produce an annual statistical report both for the overall picture of libraries in the state, and for the purpose of comparison. This is done online by an automated survey assistant, such as Bibliostat Connect,[6] that collects the information from multiple libraries using standardized questions. (Although usually performed by the librarian, LSS can be helpful in gath-ering previously generated reports; in a very small library the LSS may be performing the actual survey.) This information is then compiled into a comprehensive report. In Connecticut, the annual State Statistical Profile required information includes such factors as:

- Circulation statistics
- Program attendance
- Hours open
- Salary expenditures
- Material expenditures
- "Other" income (gifts, donations, investment income, etc.)
- Full-time-equivalent employees
- Number of Internet computers
- ILL statistics

Other statistics for comparisons include:

- Patron registration
- Library visits
- Reference questions
- Internet sessions
- Operating income/operating expenditures
- Town tax appropriation
- Program expenditures

Also used for this comparison is the adjusted equalized net grand list per capita (AENGLC) rank of a town in which the library is located—a measure of town wealth calculated annually. The lower the number is, the wealthier the town. This is an important factor when comparing libraries in different parts of the state. Besides providing data to assist libraries in evaluating their own year-to-year statistical trends, the profile provides a means of comparing library services between similar libraries. Libraries should understand, however, that some statistics vary in their consistency and accuracy.[7] While a useful tool, at this time it is limited to use only in Connecticut; other states have other means of gathering similar information.

Another benefit of the statistical profile is that it tracks statistical trends, such as circulation numbers going down, program attendance numbers going up, computer use going up, or ILL transactions going down. These trends tend to track fairly universally across the state for any given year. These numbers also are used to calculate the per capita circulation of an item—that is, how many items a resident checked out, in all age groups. Ultimately, it provides the per capita cost to circulate an item—how much it costs the library for that person to take out an item based on the total population of the service area.

Other categories for comparison include which ILS a library uses; how many FTE (full-time employees) in a particular library, salary and benefit information, and building information (number of branches, date of last construction, wheelchair accessibilities, square feet per capita served, meeting rooms, and more). There is virtually no area of the library that is not subject to reporting.

Library annual statistical reports in other states follow very similar formats, with some variation. For example, the Oregon report further breaks circulation statistics down by categories:

- First time circulation of adult materials
- Renewal of adult materials
- First time circulation of young adult materials
- Renewal of young adult materials
- First time circulation of children's materials
- Renewal of children's materials
- Number of circulations of electronic materials (not broken down by age group)
- First time circulation not broken down into adult or children's materials, etc.

This is only from the Circulation tab; they have another tab just for e-items. Their Main Data tab includes the expenditure information, ILS, square footage, Internet speed, and so on.[8] The conclusion, however, is that Oregon requires a vast amount of reporting per library to achieve the same results—a statistical breakdown of library service in that state.

Similarly, the *Public Libraries in Louisiana: Statistical Report* includes data gathered from all public libraries by the State Library of Louisiana. It is a comprehensive compilation of information about libraries, including:

- All monies available to a library from all sources of funds
- All expenditures made by the library
- Populations served
- Collections, services, and staff provided during the reporting year, and
- Performance measures[9]

No matter the state, all libraries use statistical data and reports to show how the libraries, and their services, are being used. They then evaluate the data to make improvements or adjustments as needed. There is no "judgment"—that the library in Town A is better than that in Town B. It is, however, a tool to help libraries, and their funding sources, see where they may need to better focus their efforts.

Library Planning

The benefit of keeping statistics, and studying the results, is that it helps to tell a story about your library. It can

- Evaluate the library's efficiency and effectiveness
- Identify trends in library services
- Compare with similar libraries
- Compare with state or national averages

Libraries can plan for the future by monitoring the developing trends in response to statistical data. If the report shows increased collection growth statewide, it can help to plan for the rate of collection growth in your library. This in turn helps to develop long-range planning of material and space projections. If your data show that your staff is overworked, that you are underfunded, or that your program popularity exceeds the library's capacity for space, then let the data support your position and help to advocate for the library.[10] It may be apparent that a library does not have enough FTEs per capita, but it has to be proven. Statistics support what may seem obvious to anyone who works there. They are the basis for any future planning.

Budgets

Library budgets and funding can be affected by the use of the statistics collected. For comparison purposes it can be evidence that similar libraries in similar communities are not spending as much, or are spending more, for any number of things from print material to digital content to programming. It is useful when comparing salaries of full- and part-time workers; it also shows what kind of financial support a library is getting from its municipality. They can be used, as well, to justify salary increases for librarians and support staff. When doing so, always be sure you are comparing similar libraries. The numbers are neither good nor bad—they just provide a basis for comparison.

Be aware, however, that the value of libraries cannot always be measured with numbers. If you are going to use statistics to advocate for your library, recognize that there are many other important contributions your library makes to its community that are better told in stories, anecdotes, and testimonials.

CHAPTER SUMMARY

This chapter introduced us to library statistical data—the what, why, and how of its collection and use. We examined several different kinds of reports with which LSS would be familiar, including circulation and item reports for print and electronic materials. Included were different kinds of reports such as Interlibrary Loan, and programming statistics—all integral to evaluating the library. Finally we looked at how statistics affect both future planning and budgets.

DISCUSSION QUESTIONS

1. What are collection statistics and why do we need them?
2. Explain the difference in how LSS would collect statistics for print and electronic items.
3. List several things LSS can learn from an item report.
4. Do you think that attendance statistics from library programs are important to include in the annual state library report? Why or why not?
5. Why would a current statistical report have any impact on future library planning?

ACTIVITIES

1. Describe how a library uses the ILS and other online tools to produce reports that show the use of its collections. Would you recommend any changes or improvements?
2. How does a library use these reports in making decisions about the library's collections?

NOTES

1. G. Edward Evans, Sheila S. Intner, and Jean Weihs, *Introduction to Technical Services*, 8th ed., Library and Information Science Text Series (Santa Barbara, CA: Libraries Unlimited, 2011), 60.

2. ""Public Libraries in the United States Survey Design," Institute of Museum and Library Services, accessed February 20, 2016, https://www.imls.gov/research-evaluation/data-collection/public-libraries-united-states-survey.

3. Rachel A. Fleming-May, "Practitioner Responses on the Collection and Use of Usage Statistics," *ALA TechSource*, last modified September 2010, accessed February 18, 2016, https://journals.ala.org/ltr/article/view/4401/5093.

4. G. Edward Evans and Thomas L. Carter, *Introduction to Library Public Services*, 7th ed., Library and Information Science Text Series (Westport, CT: Libraries Unlimited, 2009), 307–8.

5. "Connecticut's Public Libraries: A Statistical Profile July 2014–June 2015," LibGuides, last modified 2016, accessed February 16, 2016, http://libguides.ctstatelibrary.org/ld.php?content_id=7610605.

6. "Libraries: Information Services," Baker & Taylor, accessed February 20, 2016, http://www.btol.com/ps_details.cfm?id=222.

7. Ibid.

8. "Oregon Public Library Statistics," Oregon.gov, accessed February 16, 2016, http://www.oregon.gov/OSL/LD/pages/statsploregon.aspx.

9. *"Public Libraries in Louisiana: Statistical Report 2014,"* State Library of Louisiana, accessed February 16, 2016, http://www.state.lib.la.us/public-libraries/statistics.

10. Mark Smith, *Collecting and Using Public Library Statistics*, How-To-Do-It-Manual 56 (New York, NY: Neal-Schuman, 1996), 75.

REFERENCES, SUGGESTED READINGS, AND WEBSITES

Baker & Taylor. "Libraries: Information Services." Baker & Taylor. Accessed February 20, 2016. http://www.btol.com/ps_details.cfm?id=222.

CT State Library. "Connecticut's Public Libraries: A Statistical Profile July 2014–June 2015." LibGuides. Last modified 2016. Accessed February 16, 2016. http://libguides.ctstatelibrary.org/ld.php?content_id=7610605.

Evans, G. Edward, Sheila S. Intner, and Jean Weihs. *Introduction to Technical Services.* 8th ed. Library and Information Science Text Series. Santa Barbara, CA: Libraries Unlimited, 2011.

Fleming-May, Rachel A. "Practitioner Responses on the Collection and Use of Usage Statistics." ALA TechSource. Last modified September 2010. Accessed February 18, 2016. https://journals.ala.org/ltr/article/view/4401/5093.

Hoffert, Barbara. "Materials Breakout / Materials Survey 2015." *Library Journal.* Last modified March 2, 2015. Accessed February 18, 2016. http://reviews.libraryjournal.com/2015/03/lj-in-print/materials-breakout-materials-survey-2015/.

IMLS.gov. "Public Libraries in the United States Survey Design." Institute of Museum and Library Services. Accessed February 20, 2016. https://www.imls.gov/research-evaluation/data-collection/public-libraries-united-states-survey.

Oregon.GOV. "Oregon Public Library Statistics." Oregon.gov. Accessed February 16, 2016. http://www.oregon.gov/OSL/LD/pages/statsploregon.aspx.

Reid, Ian. "The 2014 Public Library Data Service Statistical Report: Characteristics & Trends." Public Libraries Online. Last modified June 2, 2015. Accessed February 16, 2016. http://publiclibrariesonline.org/2014/05/2013-plds/.

Smith, Mark. *Collecting and Using Public Library Statistics.* How-To-Do-It-Manual 56. New York, NY: Neal-Schuman, 1996.

State Library of Louisiana. *Public Libraries in Louisiana: Statistical Report 2014.* State Library of Louisiana. Accessed February 16, 2016. http://www.state.lib.la.us/public-libraries/statistics.

Wright, Cynthia. Interview by the author. Groton Public Library, Groton, CT. February 16, 2016.

PART III

Collection Care

CHAPTER 9

Material Preparation

LSS apply appropriate methods and techniques for accurate preparation of library resources. (ALA-LSSC Competency #9)

Topics Covered in This Chapter:

- Processing Materials
  - Ownership and Location
  - Tracking Materials
- Physical Processing
  - Print
  - Media

Key Terms:

Barcodes: Barcodes are a machine-readable code in the form of numbers and a pattern of parallel lines of varying width. The first six numbers of the barcode are the publisher's country and identification number; the next five digits represent the book's number. The last number is called a check digit, which enables the scanner to determine if the barcode was entered correctly. They are used in libraries to identify both items and patrons.

Physical processing: Physical processing means that any item a library receives must be prepared to circulate. It includes affixing barcodes, spine labels, reader interest labels, book covers, jewel cases, etc., so the item can be both protected and identified.

QR code: A QR code is the abbreviation of Quick Response code and is the trademark for a type of barcode. It has greater readability and storage capacity compared to standard UPC barcodes. QR codes consist of black modules (square dots) arranged in a square grid on a white background, which can be read by an imaging device (such as a camera or scanner).

RFID: RFID, or radio-frequency identification, is a method that combines microchips and radio technology to track items. Installed in library material, it allows the library to find an item in the building; when used for checking out materials, it can track the location of that item.

Security strips: Security strips are magnetized strips embedded in adhesive tape that are affixed between the pages, or spine and binding, of a book. If they leave the building without being desensitized they will set off the alarm in a special gate at the exit. Upon being checked back in they must be resensitized.

UPC: The UPC, or Universal Product Code, is a specific kind of barcode that is used for products other than library materials, such as stores. A UPC is a linear barcode made up of two parts: the barcode and the twelve-digit UPC number. The first six numbers of the barcode are the manufacturer's identification number. The next five digits represent the item's number.

PROCESSING MATERIALS

Preparing materials for circulation is more than just putting a cover on a book or providing access to an electronic record. There are steps to processing materials for circulation. The first, as we learned in chapter 4, is the process of receiving the materials into the library. When the shipment comes:

1. Unpack the boxes.
2. Find the packing slip (the actual invoice is almost always sent separately).
3. Check the packing slip against the contents—item for item.
4. Check the shipment itself against the order form to make sure what was received was what was ordered, and vice versa.

Once it has been established that there are no physical problems with the order, the items must be cataloged. A patron has to be able to find that item, and the first place to look is the OPAC (online public access catalog). The purpose of having a catalog is so that users can have easy access to a well-organized collection.

Ownership and Location

When processing materials there are two kinds of information that need to be added to the items: ownership, and location.

Ownership marking options of paper-based materials include:

- The traditional stamping of the library's name in indelible ink on the title page or the edges of a book
- The affixing of a bookplate with the same information on the inside cover
- The embossing or perforation of the pages

Institutions place ownership marks according to objectives, established practice, and common sense. Common practices include placing the mark where it: is easy to locate (e.g., in the same place on the same page of every book); is readily and easily visible (e.g., edge stamping of books); does not deface the item; does not obscure image or text; is on a blank side when available; is in an area of the page that is not blank/white on the other side (or the stamp will be more visible from the other side).[1]

One of the reasons we do this is to deter theft as well as to establish the ownership of the item in case it goes missing. (The argument can be made that theft happens anyway, but we do have to make every effort to identify ownership.) I have found that ownership stamps are a good way to identify materials that get lost in the process of interlibrary loan delivery, or, in one case, when books fell off the roof of a car and were rescued from the street and returned.

Nonbook materials can use stamps or labels placed where it is not harmful to the medium (on the label of individual CDs or DVDs, for example).

Location information of the item is added so it can be found in the library:

- Call numbers are usually placed on the spine of a book. This is called a "spine label."
- If the spine is too narrow, it can be placed on the front of the book, "around the corner" from where it would normally be on the spine.
- For media, place it on the front of the jewel case or DVD box, again in the same area as the spine on a book.

Tracking Materials

The nature of library materials is that they don't stay in one place. The final piece is that a system has to be in place to identify the items and to keep track of where they are. For recording and tracking information we use barcodes, now used universally in automated library systems:

1. Barcodes in books and nonprint media identify each separate item.
2. Barcodes for patrons identify each individual patron.
3. Circulation systems allow for linking of patron and item.

The barcode has been around for a while, patented in 1952 (although the technology to read them wasn't invented until several years later). "The most visually recognizable, the Universal Product Code (UPC) is a linear barcode made up of two parts: the barcode and the twelve-digit UPC number. The first six numbers of the barcode are the manufacturer's identification number. The next five digits represent the item's number. The last number is called a check digit, which enables the scanner to determine if the barcode was scanned correctly."[2] This is the barcode we use in libraries to track information on the item and the patron, and the link between both. Barcodes come in many fonts; "codabar" is mostly used in libraries and by FedEx. (The "bookland" font is based on ISBN numbers and used on book covers. Be careful which one you scan, as your system may be able to read both—but only the codabar will actually work.)

Figure 9.1. Codabar type of barcode. *Courtesy of the author*

Figure 9.2. Bookland type of barcode. *Courtesy of the author*

Barcodes are also of two types—smart and dumb. A smart barcode has been attached to an item or a person, so when scanned, the related information will appear on the screen. A dumb barcode is simply one to which no information has yet been electronically attached. (Don't pity it—think of it as having great potential!)

We are also familiar with a more recent creation called a matrix barcode—the most familiar example of which is the QR (Quick Response) code, easily read by smartphones and a favorite of advertisers, as it can provide access to websites.

There are some advantages of using barcodes in libraries:

- All data about item and patron are available via the database (for staff only).
- Limits on borrowing can be programmed in.
- Due dates of items (and subsequently, overdue items) can be specified.

Digital technology goes beyond barcodes. Marking items to avoid theft was mentioned earlier, and the conclusion was that it isn't really much of a deterrent at all.

Figure 9.3. QR code. *G. Keeler*

Many libraries will add security strips as a theft-detection device. Tattle Tape, the most recognized brand, was designed in 1970 by 3M. These are magnetized strips embedded in adhesive tape that are affixed between the pages, or spine and binding, of a book.[3] If a book equipped with a security strip leaves the building without being desensitized it will set off the alarm of a special gate at the exit. Once items are desensitized they will not set off the alarm; upon check-in they must be resensitized.

Another way to track materials is by using RFID—radio-frequency identification.[4] This method combines microchips and radio technology "tracking systems that combine security with more efficient tracking of materials throughout the library, including easier and faster charge and discharge, inventorying, and materials handling."[5] The RFID device serves the same purpose as a barcode, as it provides a unique identifier for the item. The RFID device must be scanned to retrieve the identifying information. They will work within a few feet (up to twenty feet for high-frequency devices) of the scanner. A radio-frequency identification system has three parts:

- A scanning antenna
- A transceiver with a decoder to interpret the data
- A transponder—the RFID tag—that has been programmed with information

The scanning antennas can be permanently affixed to a surface; when an RFID tag passes through the field of the scanning antenna, it detects the activation signal from the antenna. That "wakes up" the RFID chip, and it transmits the information on its microchip to be picked up by the scanning antenna.[6]

Some RFID systems have an interface between the exit sensors and the circulation system to identify the items moving out of the library. Were a patron to leave the library with a book and not be intercepted, LSS would at least know what had been taken. If the patron card also has an RFID tag, LSS will be able to determine who removed the items without properly charging them. Other RFID systems encode the circulation status on the RFID tag.[7]

There have been great strides made in RFID, as it allows libraries to streamline technology,[8] but the sense of invasion of privacy by patrons is valid. Technically, once they check out an item equipped with this technology, they are themselves being tracked. The advantages must be weighed against this concern.

PHYSICAL PROCESSING

Print

Library items have to be physically processed to make them ready to circulate; it also serves to extend the shelf life of a book. Ownership and tracking are the first steps, which were discussed earlier. If the library is not using the preprocessing service of a vendor, the LSS must then physically prepare the item. Let's start with books.

When a new book comes in, it should be examined for physical defects such as damaged covers, missing pages, or being bound upside down—all of which have been known to happen. Sometimes the pages may not be fully cut. A book that is truly defective can be returned, as long as the book is not yet processed. (If it came preprocessed and damaged, that is an exception.) Once the book has been determined to be without damage, the next step is to open the book to prevent damage to the spine. To do this the LSS would gently press several pages against the front cover of the book; then do the same to the pages in the back. This would continue until all of the pages have been pressed open.

Then the barcode would have to be placed. There are several locations to put it: inside the book on the page facing the front cover, inside the book on the page facing the back cover, or outside of the book at the top of the cover, either to the right or left, front or back. There is an argument to be made for placing the barcode on the outside, as it is easier to scan for checkout or inventory without having to open the book. Some barcodes come with the actual barcode and then a separate piece that is just the strip of numbers (which can be placed elsewhere on the same book). However, if it goes on the outside then the book first has to be covered.

Next, the spine label must be placed on the spine of the book, or if it has a paper cover, in that same location on the cover. The library should determine the height of the label placement so that they are uniform; it also makes the shelf look tidy. That is followed by a protective book jacket cover. In the event a spine label has to be placed over the plastic jacket cover, then it needs to be covered with a label protector, usually a 2 mil polyester label with rounded edges that cannot be peeled off. In some cases a library may choose to simply use transparent tape—not cellophane, as it yellows and cracks. This is to protect the spine label from coming off as the adhesive dries out.

Figure 9.4. Two kinds of polyester book covers. *Bill Memorial Library*

Book jacket covers are made of 1.5 or 2 mil polyester. They come in premeasured sheets that will accommodate a variety of standard-size books, and may be paper lined. They also come in rolls that can be cut to order. If the jacket is paper lined, then the book's paper cover (with illustrations, author's name, photo, biography, book reviews, etc.) is placed against the plastic, with the paper liner between the inside of the paper cover and ultimately, the book itself.

Using library glue or filament tape, the polyester-covered book jacket is then folded around the book and affixed into place. LSS must be aware of any illustrations on the front and back inside covers of the book as they may give information important to the text (maps, family trees, etc.). If the front and back covers have the exact same illustration, then it doesn't matter if some of it is obscured by the cover. However, if the illustrations are different, then the jacket cannot be glued directly to the book cover, but must be taped in such a way that the illustrations can be viewed.

For paperback books LSS could use either a reusable rigid or flexible polyester adjustable jacket cover that is:

- Easy to apply (to save processing time)
- Available in various heights with adjustable widths
- Providing good book protection
- Removable for reuse without book damage

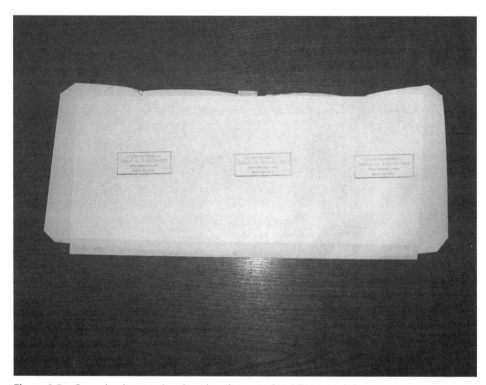

Figure 9.5.   Paper book cover placed inside polyester jacket. *Bill Memorial Library*

Or they can choose a permanent self-stick cover that:

- Is available in rigid or flexible styles
- Has precut covers that require trimming for exact fit to book
- Has a release liner that is precut and/or scored for easier removal[9]

A third option is simply to use two- to three-inch transparent, acrylic book tape to reinforce and protect the corners and spine. The final step would be to attach a security device.

In the case of serials, the basic process is the same. Ownership information must be accounted for by using a library ownership stamp or a preprinted label with the same information.

If a library uses barcodes for each issue, it has to be determined where it will go. If the library can afford it, the barcode can be permanently affixed to the issue for as long as it keeps it; some libraries only keep magazines for a defined period (one or two years) due both to storage issues and the availability of periodicals online. Alternatively, since individual magazines may only circulate for a relatively short period, LSS can attach the barcode to a separate card that will be attached to the magazine for the amount of time it is in circulation. This way, the barcode can be delinked from this item in the catalog when it is no longer useful and reused for a newer edition. Given the price of all library supplies, it may be feasible to do it this way.

There are a couple of choices to preserve the cover of the magazine before circulation. One is to use a hardcover clear magazine binder that has clear flaps in front and back to insert the covers. There is usually a metal bar to hold the spine in place. There are a variety of these on the market, from vinyl to 1.5 mil polyester.

Users need to know when to return the items. Date-due slips have traditionally been pasted into a book then stamped with the due date in ink. That way the patron only needs to look inside the book to see when it is due. Most ILS systems offer the option of printing a receipt to be given to the patron rather than stamping or marking the item itself. While it doesn't deface the book, a receipt does have a chance of getting lost. The final part of this process would be to attach a security strip, if used, as was discussed earlier.

Unfortunately LSS cannot run out to the nearest office supply shop to get the items needed for preparing materials for circulation. Book covers and magazine jackets, as well as library glue and tape, reader interest labels, and label covers, need to be ordered from companies that specialize in products for library use. These products are acid free, chemically stable, and durable. Among the leading suppliers are Demco, Brodart, and Gaylord. Their websites and catalogs offer a wide range of products suitable for the processing of library materials, and prices can vary. Through negotiated discounts (between the library and the vendor or a library cooperative and the vendor), lower prices may be secured.

Media

For nonprint materials the process is the same but the format is different. Music or books on CD or MP3, DVDs, Blu-Ray, and Playaways must all have their own records in the catalog. This is particularly important when a title is available in more

Figure 9.6. Magazine protective covers. *Bill Memorial Library*

than one format. Ownership and location markings must be used although there are limited places to put them. Barcodes are placed on the case, not on the media itself. Ownership marking will be on the cases or boxes as well as on each individual CD or DVD, in a place that will not interfere with playing the media. Adhesive labels

Figure 9.7. Media cases. *Bill Memorial Library*

are available that can be placed around the central hole in a CD or DVD. Security tapes or strips are designed just for CDs and DVDs as well. If using a date-due slip, make sure it doesn't cover the description or excerpt on the box or case.

Another layer of security for CDs and DVDs are jewel cases or locking boxes. They come with a full outer sleeve for insertion of graphics or instructions, and are bar-code, theft-strip, and RFID compatible. There are a variety of locking mechanisms that prevent the theft of discs from inside the library; for checking items out, LSS use a special key to unlock the case so the patron has access to the discs once they leave the building.[10]

Some libraries get around the problem of theft of discs by not shelving media where patrons have easy access. Instead, they shelve or display either the empty case or a facsimile cover of the item. Once that is turned in to the circulation desk for checkout, LSS either place the disc(s) in the empty case, or take the facsimile cover and hand over the actual item. This is a less costly method of preventing theft; however, once the item has left the building after checkout, the hope is that the patron will actually return the item when due.

For processing electronic titles for circulation, the library chooses and pays for materials they would like included in the system to which they subscribe, like OverDrive, for example. For an e-book to then be ready to circulate, it is up to the gurus at OverDrive to make the title electronically available on their end. Once it is available the library has no authority to change a record or even change the loan period. For a library to acquire e-books on their own to add to their collection for circulation involves their purchase and download to the library's catalog or devices. If the library circulates devices like Kindles or Nooks, they must be treated as the other nonprint media described previously—ownership markings, etc.

CHAPTER SUMMARY

In this chapter we learned about preparing materials for circulation. LSS cannot simply unpack a box of books, CDs, or other media and place them on the shelf for patrons to borrow. The items have to be marked for ownership so they can be identified outside of the library, and equipped with barcodes to track them in the catalog. Finally they are physically processed using the appropriate materials that will both protect the item and sustain its usability. Electronic materials and their handling were also discussed.

DISCUSSION QUESTIONS

1. What is a QR code, and how does it differ from a barcode? If you have used a QR code, what did you find?
2. Libraries use RFID to keep track of their collection. How is this done? Do you agree with their use or do you see a potential for misuse?
3. Name some of the items used to physically prepare an item for circulation.
4. The materials that are needed to physically process items can be costly. Do you think it is worth it, and why?
5. Library materials in all formats are subject to theft. What are some things a library can do to deter theft?
6. How does a library make electronic books available for circulation?

ACTIVITIES

1. Using a flowchart, narrative, or presentation, describe the methods a library uses to prepare books, serials, and one nonprint item, for circulation.
2. Create a guide for a new LSS whose duties include preparing library resources for circulation.
3. Using a free app available online (such as GOQRme, Visualead, or QR Stuff), create your own QR code for an item or site.

NOTES

1. "Ownership Marking of Paper-Based Materials," Library of Congress-Preservation-Collection Care, accessed February 24, 2016, http://www.loc.gov/preservation/care/marking.html.

2. "Barcode: The Ultimate Guide to Barcodes," *Wasp Buzz*, accessed February 24, 2016, http://www.waspbarcode.com/buzz/barcode/.

3. "Magnetic Strips Processing," video file, 36 sec., YouTube, posted March 30, 2010, accessed February 25, 2016, https://www.youtube.com/watch?v=plQk2czLcQ8.

4. "AM and RF security tag basics and deactivation," video file, 4 min. 9 sec., YouTube, posted by Will Phoneman, December 13, 2013, accessed February 26, 2016, https://www.youtube.com/watch?v=1w9RK92dOlk&ebc=ANyPxKrqNee55g6LjPv3R6D14R8vI.

5. Richard W. Boss, "RFID Technology for Libraries," *ALA Technotes*, last modified May 14, 2004, accessed February 24, 2016, http://www.ala.org/PrinterTemplate.cfm?Section=technotes&Template=/ContentManagement/HTMLDisplay.cfm&ContentID=68138.

6. "What Is RFID?," *Technovelgy*, http://www.technovelgy.com/ct/technology-article.asp.

7. Boss, "RFID Technology for Libraries."

8. Phil Morehart, "RFID to the Rescue," *American Libraries*, last modified May 21, 2015, accessed February 24, 2016, http://americanlibrariesmagazine.org/2015/05/21/rfid-to-the-rescue/.

9. "Paperback Book Protection," Brodart, accessed February 25, 2016, http://www.Shopbrodart.Com/Book-Protection/.

10. "Media Supplies," Brodart, accessed February 25, 2016, http://www.shopbrodart.com/media-storage/.

REFERENCES, SUGGESTED READINGS, AND WEBSITES

"AM and RF security tag basics and deactivation." Video file, 4 min. 9 sec. YouTube. Posted by Will Phoneman, December 13, 2013. Accessed February 26, 2016. https://www.youtube.com/watch?v=1w9RK92dOlk&ebc=ANyPxKrqNee55g6LjPv3R6D14R8vI.

Block, Rick J. "Authority Control: What It Is and Why It Matters." PowerPoint presentation. PPT File Search. Accessed February 23, 2016. http://pptfilesearch.com/single/148373/authority-control-what-it-is-and-why-it-matters.

Boss, Richard W. "RFID Technology for Libraries." *ALA Technotes*. Last modified May 14, 2004. Accessed February 24, 2016. http://www.ala.org/PrinterTemplate.cfm?Section=technotes&Template=/ContentManagement/HTMLDisplay.cfm&ContentID=68138.

Brodart. "Media Supplies." Brodart. Accessed February 25, 2016. http://www.shopbrodart.com/media-storage/.

———. "Paperback Book Protection." Brodart. Accessed February 25, 2016. http://www.shopbrodart.com/book-protection/.

Evans, G. Edward, Sheila S. Intner, and Jean Weihs. *Introduction to Technical Services*. 8th ed. Library and Information Science Text Series. Santa Barbara, CA: Libraries Unlimited, 2011.

Florida International University. "Authority Control." Florida International University Libraries. Accessed February 23, 2016. https://library.fiu.edu/about-us/cataloging/authority-control.

Library of Congress. "Ownership Marking of Paper-Based Materials." Library of Congress-Preservation-Collection Care. Accessed February 24, 2016. http://www.loc.gov/preservation/care/marking.html.

"Magnetic Strips Processing." Video file, 36 sec. YouTube. Posted March 31, 2010. Accessed February 26, 2016. https://www.youtube.com/watch?v=plQk2czLcQ8.

Morehart, Phil. "RFID to the Rescue." *American Libraries*. Last modified May 21, 2015. Accessed February 24, 2016. http://americanlibrariesmagazine.org/2015/05/21/rfid-to-the-rescue/.

"Processing Library Materials—Book Jackets." Video file, 7 min. 57 sec. YouTube. Posted by Chris Rippel, October 16, 2008. Accessed February 26, 2016. https://www.youtube.com/watch?v=U8hb-dbb-OI.

Rach. "Basic Library Procedures: Processing Library Materials." *Living in the Library World* blog. Last modified January 7, 2009. Accessed February 23, 2016. http://livinginthelibraryworld. blogspot.com/2009/01/basic-library-procedures-processing.html.

"RFID Tagging at the Library, Day 1." Video file. YouTube. Posted May 1, 2014. Accessed March 29, 2016. https://www.youtube.com/watch?v=QcuA-GW3sFs.

Technovelgy LCC. "What Is RFID?" *Technovelgy.* http://www.technovelgy.com/ct/technology -article.asp.

Wasp Barcode Technologies. "Barcode: The Ultimate Guide to Barcodes." *Wasp Buzz.* Accessed February 24, 2016. http://www.waspbarcode.com/buzz/barcode/.

CHAPTER 10

Preservation and Security

LSS know the principles and basic practices regarding the preservation of library resources.
(ALA-LSSC Competency #8)

Key Terms:

Conservation: Conservation is a specific term used in the field of preservation that refers to the physical care given to individual items within collections. This ranges from the repair of circulating collections to the restoration of rare materials. This should only be done by recognized conservators from certified programs.

Digitization: Digitization is the process of converting materials to a digital, or electronic, format. Digitizing books is already available in the form of e-books from commercial publishers; it can be considered a form of preservation in that once a book, image, or document is converted to this format it may be used to replace the more fragile paper-based original.

Disaster Planning: Disaster planning means creating a working plan for how the library would respond in the event of a severe emergency, such as weather-related issues, fire, and water damage. It includes having an emergency kit of supplies and a list of contacts, and it addresses prevention as well as remediation.

HVAC: HVAC refers to a heating, ventilation, and air-conditioning system. It controls the temperature and humidity of a building to maintain a constant rate. This is an environment critical to paper-based collections and should be in all libraries.

Preservation: Preservation is a term in general use to define activities that will prolong the life of materials by particular attention to solutions concerning entire collections. It includes concerns about the environment, handling, and storage. This can be done by staff trained in a few basic concepts.

Repair: Repair is the *physical treatment carried out upon circulation collections* to prolong their usable life. It includes cover repairs, mending pages and bindings, and cleaning pages. This can be done by anyone trained in the correct methods

RH: RH stands for relative humidity. Humidity is the water vapor in the air. It is directly related to temperature and should be at about a 45 percent level in a library at all times. Too much fluctuation in either direction can damage paper.

PRINT MATERIALS

The majority of materials in a school or public library are still paper based; we will begin the topic of preservation, then, by addressing print materials.

Any discussion about preservation of books and materials brings up the question of the value of old books. Being old does not necessarily mean a book is valuable; in many cases the value of an old book is largely intrinsic—that is, it means something special to the owner. There is definitely value in that. There are, however, ways to tell if an old book does have monetary value, including numerous websites that allow you to look up your book in relation to similar ones for sale, or those that have sold. Dealers in antique books are also good resources. What they will tell you is that what matters most is its condition.

The following is a bit of "tongue in cheek advice" which is adapted from an old issue of *Bookseller* magazine:[1]

How to Reduce the Value of Your Books
1. When you get a new book, throw away the jacket. In twenty-five or thirty years, when it turns out this was a rare and collectible first edition or a now famous author, the lack of a dust jacket will drop the value from $100 to $5.

2. Open it. Place the spine on a firm surface, open the book in the middle and press down. You will experience a soul-satisfying thrill as the spine snaps.

3. When you get interrupted, dog ear the page or turn it upside down and place a weight on it so it cannot escape.

4. Always underline, in ink or yellow highlighter.

5. Be sure to cut out and frame any good illustration. If it is a borrowed book, write in the margin about what a pretty picture it was.

6. Write in the margins. Unless you are famous, it ruins the value.

7. The inside pages are great places to store things: four leaf clovers, newspaper clippings (20 years later this will be a lovely brown patch on the adjacent page), cancelled checks, money.

8. Have your children or grandchildren exercise their creative talent with crayons, ink, lipstick, dirty fingers, etc., on the end papers and title page.

9. If you have a wobbly chair, select a book of the proper thickness and shim the chair with it.

10. When you put your books on the shelf, jam them in as tightly as possible. Then when you want it, place an index finger in the top and pull. This will enable you to split the top of the spine.

11. A special note about reading while eating: put the book in the position normally occupied by the plate. Then when you eat a sloppy joe or hamburger, the open pages of the book will catch the drippings and save the tablecloth.

12. Store your books so the sun can fade the spines or covers, or both. If you have to store them for a long time, put them in a garage, a hot attic, or a damp shed. Roaches, termites, silverfish and other critters love these places. Dampness also promotes mildew and gives your books that wonderful musty smell.

With that in mind, preservation means more than just taking care of, or "preserving," materials. It means taking several areas into account, including prevention. There are three distinct areas of preservation of paper-based materials:

Conservation is a specific term used in the field of preservation that refers to the *physical care given to individual items within collections*. This ranges from the repair of circulating collections to the restoration of rare materials. This should only be done by recognized conservators from certified programs. Places like the American Institute for Conservation of Historic & Artistic Works,[2] in Washington, D.C., or Northeast Document Conservation Center,[3] in Andover, Massachusetts, can provide the training and guidance for such work.

Preservation is a term in general use to define activities that will prolong the life of materials by particular attention to *solutions concerning entire collections*. It includes concerns about the environment, handling, and storage. Unlike conservation, this can be done by staff trained in a few basic concepts using proper preservation materials.

Repair is the *physical treatment carried out upon circulation collections* to prolong their usable life. It includes cover repairs, mending pages and bindings, and cleaning pages. This can be done by anyone trained in the correct methods, and will be covered in the next chapter.

One way to preserve fragile materials is to use protective enclosures that conform to preservation standards. These include boxes, folders, and sleeves that are acid free,

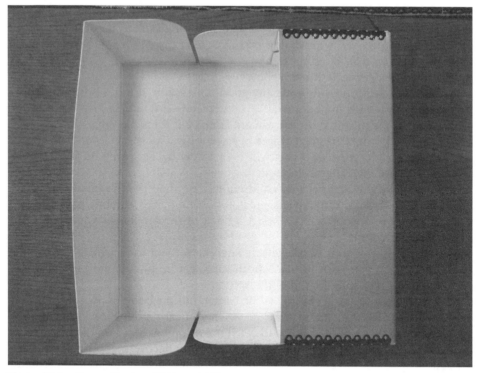

Figure 10.1.   Preservation box. *Bill Memorial Library*

and can protect items damaged from heavy use, general wear, brittle paper, or the environment. Materials can also be reformatted using microfilm, microfiche, and photocopy[4] (although the light used to do so can also be damaging).

THE ENVIRONMENT

Elements That Affect Paper

Paper has traditionally been produced by wood pulp broken down by acidic chemicals, which, combined with poor environmental conditions, creates self-destructing books with a shelf life of only about fifty years. Most books produced between 1850 and 1930 have this problem. If the corner of a page breaks after being folded up to three times, it is too brittle to repair. They can, as mentioned above, be reformatted using microfilm or permanent durable paper.

While paper today is also made from wood pulp, the difference is that often cotton, linen, or hemp is added, which preserves its longevity. During the pulping process, lignin, an acid found in wood that contributes to brittleness, is removed from the paper. Modern paper has a neutral ph of about 7,[5] which increases its longevity as well.

The Northeast Document Conservation Center offers reproducible preservation leaflets that cover virtually everything to do with care and handling of your collection. Relevant examples include Leaflet 2.1, "Temperature, Relative Humidity, Light and Air Quality: Basic Guidelines for Preservation"; Leaflet 2.2, "Monitoring Temperature and Relative Humidity"; and Leaflet 4.1, "Storage Methods and Handling Practices." Their website is a source of valuable advice helpful to the LSS.[6]

Factors that contribute to the deterioration of paper-based materials include:

1. **Temperature**: Physical and chemical deterioration is accelerated by high temperatures and inadequate humidity. Most experts agree that a temperature of 68–70°F is ideal. A rule of thumb is that for every ten-degree rise in temperature, the life of acidic book paper is halved.
2. **Relative humidity**, or **RH**: Humidity is the water vapor in the air. It is related to temperature; as the temperature rises, the air has a greater capacity to hold moisture. If the humidity is too low, it will dry out paper. If the temperature is too high there is increased moisture in the air, and mold can form. Mold can infiltrate an entire shelf within seventy-two hours. A reasonable RH is around 45 percent with little fluctuation. As an example, a local school library was closed for the summer when the HVAC system failed. With no air conditioning, and no one to discover this until school started up in the fall, every item in the library was covered in mold.
3. **Light**: While all light is potentially destructive to paper, the worst is ultraviolet, or UV light. Fluorescent lights, often found in commercial buildings, and sunlight from uncovered windows are especially damaging. Strong light fades covers and bindings and speeds chemical deterioration. A good example is a newspaper left in the sun—after a day or two it is faded and yellowed. It is important to eliminate or reduce strong sources of light, or use UV filters.
4. **Dust**: Good Housekeeping is not just a magazine! Dust, dirt, and air pollution all contribute to the deterioration of paper. All HVAC systems should have filters installed for particulates, and be cleaned on a regular basis. Floors, shelves, and books should be dusted as part of the library's ongoing maintenance plan. While the thought of dusting all of those library books can be daunting, it can be scheduled on a rotating basis to break it up. Or dust every time you shelve! Using a soft rag or feather duster, a good way to dust a book is to hold it firmly at the spine with the fore edge parallel to the floor, and flick the dust away. A small vacuum can also be used.

Shelving, Housing, Care, and Handling

Library materials can be damaged simply by shelving or removing them from the stacks. Here are some tips to minimize the impact:

1. Books should be properly placed on carts to avoid having them fall over or hit shelves.
2. Once on the shelf, books should be upright and supported well on both sides.
3. Oversized volumes may need to be laid flat, no more than three to a stack.
4. Books should be shelved spine down to avoid loosening the text block.
5. Don't drop them!
6. As tempting as it is, don't pull a book off the shelf by its head cap—that can loosen or rip the spine. Instead, nudge adjoining books back so the entire book can be firmly grasped.

Although pages in books can be photocopied, be very careful how it is done. A copier with an edge platen—one that allows the side of the book to hang over while the opposite page is being copied—is preferable to a copier that requires the book to be laid facedown. This can stress the spine and binding.

Similarly, books on display need to be supported to reduce stress to joints and spines. This is a great marketing tool, and there are a number of book display holders available that allow the book to be cradled. If a book is being displayed open to highlight text or artwork, be sure to turn the pages daily to minimize exposure to light.

Yet another hazard is the library book return—a receptacle that allows books to be dropped into a bin. The best book returns have float trays or spring loaded floors that rise and fall with the weight. Regardless, falling books can cause bent or torn pages, loosened bindings, and broken joints. Some bins may need a layer of padding to soften the fall. They should be made of aluminum or stainless steel and be bolted down (if outdoors), and have removable carts to get the items out easily.

Book return bins can be targets of mischief and vandalism as well. Both outdoor, and through the wall, bins can be recipients of, at best, a melted ice cream cone. Indoor bins can be potentially more dangerous as the Danbury Public Library in Connecticut found out when an object on fire was dropped into their book drop in 1996, causing $25 million in damages.[7]

Physical Treatment

LSS at the circulation desk play an important role in keeping collections safe. Some things that they can do include:

- If stamping books, do it on a flat surface to avoid damage to the spine.
- LSS can advise patrons on protecting materials in wet weather (keep a supply of plastic grocery bags to offer them).
- Above all, they should advise patrons not to make repairs on their own.[8]

In a bad news/good news scenario, circulated materials are damaged through use, or are poorly made to begin with. Fortunately there are a number of repairs that LSS can carry out on these materials, which is the subject of the next chapter.

NONPRINT MATERIALS

The guidelines for preserving nonprint or non-paper-based material are pretty much the same. There are some differences, however:

- Film-based media ideally should be stored in cooler temperatures and lower RH (it deteriorates rapidly over 80°F)—which may be hard to do in a library without special rooms to accommodate the changes.
  - Films should be stored in canisters.
  - All film-based media should be handled using gloves to avoid fingerprints.
  - All film should be stored away from strong light levels, in acid-free boxes or envelopes.

Figure 10.2. Through-the-wall (interior) book drop. *Groton Public Library*

Figure 10.3. Freestanding outdoor library book drop.

- Magnetic material deteriorates at temperatures over 90°F, and is destroyed by exposure to computers and certain kinds of electrical equipment.
  - ○ Fortunately, this kind of media—in the form of sound or video cassettes—is no longer actively collected by libraries.
- CDs and DVDs have a longer shelf life, but can be damaged by scratches and oils.
  - ○ Common sense dictates using clean hands, and not touching the surfaces of the discs.

In the case of a water emergency, discs can be rinsed in distilled water and dried with a soft cloth, then be run through the disc repair machine. They may also need to be professionally resurfaced at a shop that specializes in CDs and DVDs.

Film is the only nonprint media that has the potential to be irreparably damaged. Film or filmstrips should be unrolled and looped around a clothesline to dry; photographs should be laid out on toweling in low temperatures and humidity to let air dry. They will stick to each other if stacked; consulting with a conservator may be necessary.

The hope, of course, is that the equipment used to "read" this material will still be available. Floppy discs are no longer useful as there are no more floppy drives on computers. Maybe someday the USB port will go the way of the disc drive. It is impossible to foresee what new technologies may replace what we now have making the information we save today unreadable tomorrow.

DIGITIZATION

Digitization is the process of converting materials to a digital, or electronic, format. Digitized books are readily available in the form of e-books from commercial publishers. But digitization can be considered a form of preservation in that once a book, image, or document is converted to this format it can replace the more fragile paper-based original.

For many years printed materials have been converted to a microform platform. Invented in the late 1800s, microfilming, or microphotography, didn't come into commercial use until the 1920s. Subsequent improvements to microfilm and its optical readers assured its use. "Preservation microfilming quietly maintains its status as a highly valued and widely practiced preservation reformatting strategy."[9] An advantage is that it can be read with the naked eye using good light and magnification (in the event a microform reader is not available). Microforms come in many types and follow strict standards of preservation.

The conversion of books to an electronic format is a newer concept by comparison. The Gutenberg Project was founded in 1971 by Michael Hart to encourage the creation and distribution of e-books, and currently has 50,000 titles available. They are in the public domain, as their copyrights have expired; the site offers a wide variety of titles in e-book, CD, and DVD downloadable formats.

In 2004 Google launched Google Print, an enormous effort to digitize the collections of several major university libraries, both current and out of print books. It was subsequently renamed Google Books, or Google Book Search. Not without controversy, this enterprise met with resistance and lawsuits from publishers and authors about the issue of copyright violation. After years of litigation, Google Books became legal in 2015.[10] "In addition to contracting with publishers of current imprints, the project involved a Library Partners program to scan tens of millions of books from major libraries around the world, and apply full-text indexing to them, making them full searchable. To date, Google has scanned and indexed over 12 million volumes . . . and the list of participating libraries has grown to about 30, from around the world."[11]

The digitization of millions of items serves as the ultimate form of preservation, assuring that regardless of their condition, this material will be accessible to generations to come. That assumes, of course, that access to digital databases remains viable.

SECURITY

Emergencies

Emergencies are part of your preservation program. If ignored, small problems can become big problems. There are degrees of emergencies, and LSS need to know what to do in each situation.

Water emergencies can range from a broken pipe to a leaky roof. For years the staff at one library held their breath every time there was a heavy rainstorm, as it was well known by all which windows leaked, and where the rain would come in through parts of the ceiling. As water emergencies can also include overflowing sinks and toilets, it is important to know where the shut-off valves are for each one. Leaky pipes can cause extensive and irreparable harm to collections, but precautions can be taken. Roofs and flashings should be inspected regularly and repaired or replaced as needed. Gutters and drains should be cleaned frequently.[12]

If books and papers do get wet there are several ways to dry them: air drying, commercial dehumidification, and several ways of freeze drying. Which method is used depends on the number of books, space to dry them, and cost. Identifying and contacting experts listed in your recovery plan can help with that decision, as it will have become a much larger job than can be carried out by library staff.

1. Fire emergencies can also range from the incidental to the catastrophic. Libraries can have electrical malfunctions that result in small fires as well as small kitchen or microwave incidents that can be resolved with a fire extinguisher. Several fire-suppression methods are available, and every institution should have at least one method in operation. Automatic sprinklers are now considered by most fire safety professionals, librarians, archivists, and conservators to be the best protection from fire for libraries and archives. The preferred type of sprinkler system depends upon the institution's objectives. Before making a choice, staff should consult an experienced fire safety engineer who is familiar with libraries and archives and with current developments in the field.[13]
2. Fungus can also be considered an emergency. It occurs from damp, warm environments, which speed up the growth of mold and mildew. Not only is it bad for books and materials, but it is bad for health. It helps to have a good air filtration system, but prevention (proper heat/humidity) is most important.
3. Biological agents pose a serious threat to libraries in the form of bugs and rodents. This is where controlling conditions in the library can prevent or minimize their damage.

Keeping the library clean and free from food and drinks is an important component of preventing pests.

Learn to recognize the signs of pests:

- Book lice are pinhead-sized and grayish white, and they like dark dusty corners where they can eat book paste, glue, and fungus.
- Book worms are actually beetle larvae; they burrow through covers and lay eggs on pages. The warning signs of book worms include dust on the shelves (which is *not* really dust) and book pages that are stuck together.
- Silverfish only come out at night; if you are finding lacy holes on a page, then that is a telltale sign that you have silverfish. They like glue and paper.
- Cockroaches eat everything. Signs that they may be among you include discoloration on the shelves and brown liquid across the pages.
- Termites eat wood, and will eat books while they are at it. It helps to have metal shelves.
- Mice and rats will also eat books and leave behind their "calling cards" as well, that can transmit disease.[14]

If you find an infested book, isolate it immediately and seal it in a plastic bag; then place the bag in the freezer for up to forty-eight hours to kill the pests. Professional help should be sought.

A somewhat new pest that has turned up in recent years is the bedbug:

Libraries are not ideal environments for the tiny oval-shaped Cimex lectularius, which prefer to be near sleeping people. However, a number of public and academic libraries from California to New York have been challenged in recent years by bed bugs, having to close several buildings while a pest control company treated furnishings and books. That's because bed bugs can stow away on books, clothing, and belongings such as backpacks, then be transported to other locations, including libraries. . . . Bed bugs arrive at libraries through materials returned to book drops as well as on patrons' bags or clothing. Once inside, they can hide on shelves and in furnishings, but they will seek out people on which to snack.[15]

Since heat kills them, there are a number of specially designed heated boxes or bags in which an affected book can be placed for treatment. The best defense being a good offense, some libraries buy a heat box for this purpose and have the library inspected by a licensed pest control company as a preventative measure. Finding any evidence of pests does not necessarily mean there is an infestation, but common sense would require that a professional be brought in for a thorough inspection.

Disaster Planning

The most important part of disaster planning is *prevention*. "Emergency preparedness is an important component of overall preservation planning. An emergency preparedness plan should cover all hazards, including water and fire, that pose a reasonable threat to collections. A systematically organized, formally written plan enables you to respond efficiently and quickly to an emergency, minimizing danger to staff and damage to collections and the building. Such a plan should cover preventive measures as well as recovery procedures."[16]

Before disaster strikes, make sure that data is being consistently backed up and stored off-site. Fluorescent lights that contain PCBs should be replaced, and if the building contains asbestos, it should be professionally removed, as it could be a nightmare if it becomes wet or airborne.

Preventative measures may also protect the library as the insurance company may not cover the costs of damage caused by a library's inaction. Insurance adjustments should be part of the written disaster plan considering such things as replacement versus recovery costs (the cost to dry material may range from $.45 to $.60/cubic foot, or $5 to $10/book; replacement cost is much higher).

While water, fire, fungus, and pests pose emergencies of varying degrees, libraries should be prepared for the worst. Having a disaster plan in place is the first step and it should have an outline of emergency procedures for the staff to follow.

Start by having a floor plan noting the exits, fire alarms, and fire extinguishers:

- All library staff, from the director on down, should know where the utilities come into the library, such as the electrical panel and water shut-off valves.

- They should have the phone numbers to the police and fire departments, and know where the insurance papers are located.
- This should all be written down on an emergency list and posted, as well as distributed electronically to all staff.

Then be sure to have a list of priorities, as there may not be enough time to get everything out:

1. The first priority is people—clear the building!
2. Then get the irreplaceable materials needed to run the library even if they are not sensitive to water, such as fiscal records and other vital operating records that are not stored electronically (and backed up off-site).
3. Take the materials that cannot be subjected to water, such as old photos.
4. Get the material needed to maintain the integrity of the collection, such as the shelf list if it is not already stored electronically.
5. If there is time, get the material that would be nice to have, but not crucial to the integrity of the collection.
6. If possible unplug all of the computers and equipment to prevent damage from a potential power surge.

Every library should have a basic emergency supply kit that everyone on staff knows where to find. It should include:

TEXTBOX 10.1 EMERGENCY SUPPLY KIT CONTENTS

a. The floor plan of the entire building
b. Plastic sheeting to cover the stacks in case of water damage
c. Rubber gloves and boots
d. Air filter masks
e. Flashlights
f. Disposable camera with film, or digital camera
g. The list of consultants and specialists to help with recovery, including the insurance company

Should your library be unfortunate enough to experience a true emergency, here is a summary:

a. In a water emergency, shut off the water or plug the leak.
b. In a fire emergency, pull the fire alarm and/or call 911 and evacuate the building.
c. Contact the response team, disaster recovery contractors, and the insurance company.
d. If water is flowing, cover materials. When it stops, clean it up, remove wet materials.
e. In a fire, gather supplies, wait for permission to enter, pack up damaged material as planned.

After the emergency is over, check with authorities about when you can reenter the building to begin recovery.

CHAPTER SUMMARY

Library materials in all formats must be preserved. This chapter presents conservation as the umbrella under which preservation and repair fall, and how it affects print and nonprint materials. The environment is a major factor in the preservation of materials including temperature, humidity, light, and dust. The physical treatment of materials as well as their care and handling play a large part in retaining the integrity of library materials. Emergencies and disaster plans are addressed as a worst-case scenario; and digitization is presented as another solution to the important issue of preservation of materials.

DISCUSSION QUESTIONS

1. Explain the differences between conservation, preservation, and repair, paying particular attention to what LSS can do in the library to help.
2. Describe the variety of environmental factors that can stress or damage material in a library collection.
3. Take an informal survey of the library book drops in your area, both outdoor and through the wall. What differences do you observe, and what suggestions could you make to improve them?
4. Having food and drinks in the library can attract pests. What else could the LSS do to prevent these infestations?
5. Your local area is expecting a major weather event. What can LSS do to prevent damage, and to make recovery easier?
6. What is digitization and what role does it play in the preservation of library materials?

ACTIVITIES

1. Make arrangements to visit several libraries and ask what environmental factors they take into consideration, such as: the temperature and RH; the kind of lighting they use; if they maintain a regular schedule for dusting; and how they address pest management. Write a one-page essay with your findings.
2. Taking into account all facets of library operations, create a sample disaster plan. What would it include?

NOTES

1. "How to Reduce the Value of Your Books," *Bookseller*, July 21, 1999, 4.
2. "About us," American Institute for Conservation of Historic & Artistic Works, last modified 2015, accessed March 8, 2016, http://www.conservation-us.org/about-us#.Vt8e4fkrKUk.

3. "Northeast Document Conservation Center," NEDCC, accessed March 8, 2016, https://www.nedcc.org/.

4. Sally Buchanan, *Preserving Library Resources: A Guide for Staff* (Pittsburgh, PA: Oakland Library Consortium, 1990), 2–3.

5. "Preservation FAQs," Amigos Library Services, accessed March 8, 2016, https://www.amigos.org/node/79.

6. Northeast Document Conservation Center, NEDCC Preservation Leaflets, accessed March 28, 2016, https://www.nedcc.org/free-resources/preservation-leaflets/overview.

7. Jack Cavanaugh, "A Library Fire Spurs Copycat Fears," *New York Times*, last modified March 19, 1996, accessed March 8, 2016, http://www.nytimes.com/1996/03/17/nyregion/a-library-fire-spurs-copycat-fears.html.

8. Buchanan, *Preserving Library Resources*, 4–7.

9. Northeast Document Conservation Center, "Leaflet 6.1: Microfilm and Microfiche," NEDCC Preservation Leaflets, accessed March 28, 2016, https://www.nedcc.org/free-resources/preservation-leaflets/6.-reformatting/6.1-microfilm-and-microfiche.

10. Robinson Meyer, "After 10 Years, Google Books Is Legal," *Atlantic*, last modified October 25, 2015, accessed March 28, 2016, http://www.theatlantic.com/technology/archive/2015/10/fair-use-transformative-leval-google-books/411058/.

11. "Google Books," Stanford University Libraries, accessed March 28, 2016, https://library.stanford.edu/projects/google-books.

12. Sherelyn Ogden, "3.1 Protection from Loss: Water and Fire Damage, Biological Agents, Theft, and Vandalism," Northeast Document Conservation Center, accessed March 9, 2016, https://www.nedcc.org/free-resources/preservation-leaflets/3.-emergency-management/3.1-protection-from-loss-water-and-fire-damage,-biological-agents,-theft,-and-vandalism.

13. Ibid.

14. Molly Edmonds, "Book Care: Protecting Books from Mice, Mold and Moisture," How Stuff Works, accessed March 9, 2016, http://home.howstuffworks.com/home-improvement/remodeling/home-library3.htm.

15. Marta Murvosh, "Don't Let the Book Bugs Bite," *Library Journal* 138, no. 12 (July 1, 2013): 32.

16. Ogden, "3.1 Protection from Loss."

REFERENCES, SUGGESTED READINGS, AND WEBSITES

Alleman, Gayle A. "How DVDs Work." How Stuff Works: Tech. Last modified 2016. Accessed March 4, 2016. http://electronics.howstuffworks.com/dvd2.htm.

Baird, Brian. Interview. Bridgeport National Bindery, Agawam, MA. December 15, 2015.

"Bookbinding." In *Columbia Electronic Encyclopedia*, 1. 6th ed. New York: Columbia University Press, 2015.

Book Repair: Spine Repair with Hollow Tube. Photograph. Smith Library, Eastern CT State University. November 24, 2015. Accessed March 4, 2016.

Book Repair: Supplies and Tools. Photograph. Smith Library, Eastern CT State University. November 24, 2015. Accessed March 4, 2016.

Book Repair: Tipping in Pages. Photograph. Smith Library, Eastern CT State University. November 24, 2015. Accessed March 4, 2016.

Brodart Co. "Library supplies: Book Care and Repair." Brodart. Accessed March 4, 2016. http://www.shopbrodart.com/library-supplies-school-supplies/book-care/?=.

Dartmouth College. "A Simple Book Repair: Guiding Principles." Dartmouth College Library. Last modified January 1, 2012. Accessed March 1, 2016. http://www.dartmouth.edu/~library/preservation/repair/guideprinc.html?mswitch-redir=classic.

Demco. "Library Supplies: Book Repair." Demco. Accessed March 4, 2016. http://demco.com/goto?PNHC68&intcmp=CN_C68.

Eberhart, George M. *The Whole Library Handbook 3*. 3rd ed. Chicago, IL: American Library Association, 2000.

An Introduction to Book Repair. Syracuse, NY: Gaylord, 1998.

Ison, John. "The Book Doctor Is In: Book Repair ASAP." Ideas + Inspiration from Demco. Last modified June 23, 2015. Accessed March 3, 2016. http://ideas.demco.com/blog/book-repair-series-2/.

Meyer, Robinson. "After 10 Years, Google Books Is Legal." *Atlantic*. Last modified October 25, 2015. Accessed March 28, 2016. http://www.theatlantic.com/technology/archive/2015/10/fair-use-transformative-leval-google-books/411058/.

Northeast Document Conservation Center. "Leaflet 6.1: Microfilm and Microfiche." NEDCC Preservation Leaflets. Accessed March 28, 2016. https://www.nedcc.org/free-resources/preservation-leaflets/6.-reformatting/6.1-microfilm-and-microfiche.

Project Gutenberg Literary Archive Foundation. "Free ebooks by Project Gutenberg." Project Gutenberg. Last modified February 21, 2016. Accessed March 28, 2016. https://www.gutenberg.org/.

Stanford University. "Google Books." Stanford University Libraries. Accessed March 28, 2016. https://library.stanford.edu/projects/google-books.

UCLA. "Microfilm: A Brief History." Southern Region Library Facility UCLA. Accessed March 28, 2016. http://www.srlf.ucla.edu/exhibit/text/WhatIs.htm.

Verheyen, Peter D., and Marianne Hanley. "Book Repair Basics for Libraries." Association for Library Collections & Technical Services (ALCTS). Accessed March 3, 2016. http://downloads.alcts.ala.org/ce/091411book_repair_basics.pdf.

WikiHow. "How to Fix a Scratched CD." WikiHow. Accessed March 4, 2016. http://www.wikihow.com/Fix-a-Scratched-CD.

YouTube. "AbeBooks Explains the Parts of a Book." YouTube. Last modified September 28, 2011. Accessed March 4, 2016. https://www.youtube.com/watch?v=DQyntYcGwik.

———. "Library Collection Care Videos." YouTube. Last modified December 11, 2013. Accessed March 4, 2016. https://www.youtube.com/playlist?list=PL9876A71BE2C6220C.

CHAPTER 11

Basic Material Repair

LSS know the principles and basic practices regarding the preservation of library resources.
(ALA-LSSC Competency #8)

Topics Covered in This Chapter:
- Book Repair Overview
  - Anatomy of a Book
  - Caring for Books
  - Tools and Materials
- Principles of Repair
  - Marked and Torn Pages
  - Page Tip-ins
  - Cover Reattachment
  - Hinges, Corners, and Spines
- Binderies
- Nonbook Material

Key Terms:

Bindery: A book bindery is a facility that rebinds, repairs, and produces print books. Rebinding a book means replacing a damaged cover with a new one, either by reusing the original artwork or making a new plain cover. They can also add hard covers to paperback books. They usually have the capability of creating a book from scratch, as well as providing print-on-demand services.

Bone folder: Bone folders, originally made of bone, are now available in plastic. They are usually white, oblong, and come in several sizes—usually six to seven inches long, an inch or so wide, and three-fourths of an inch thick. The edges are rounded. They are used to apply pressure when making creases on paper or pressing down glued surfaces.

Expediency: Expediency means that almost any non-brittle book can be repaired, given enough time and the proper equipment. Simple book repair implies that the repair will not take hours or days of staff time.

Hinges: Hinges are the portion of the book closest to the spine that allows the book to be opened and closed. When a book is dropped or otherwise stressed, the hinges can come loose or even broken. This can also happen from age as glue dries out. They need to be repaired to hold the book together.

Print-on-demand services (POD): POD is a service that allows books to be printed one at a time as needed. Binderies offer this service, as do a number of online services. A bindery can produce one, or a series of books in any quantity, using the POD machine.

PVA: PVA stands for polyvinyl acetate, a water-based, pH-neutral, and acid-free adhesive. It is white but dries clear and quickly. PVA is the standard in library glue for repairs and binding.

Quick and dirty repair: "Quick and dirty" repairs are those that can be done with a minimum of effort, but with care and skill to get the materials back on the shelf. They include cleaning pages, mending tears, and fixing loose hinges.

Reversibility: Reversibility is the principle that any treatment applied to a book should be reversible; that is, it can be undone easily at a later date. This would be done if newer or better repairs can be performed; or if the book is of significant value (as repairs lower the value).

Spine: The spine of a book is its backbone. It is attached to the front and back covers to form the case for the text block to fit into. If the spine is broken or pulls away, the entire book can fall apart. Spines can also be damaged by inappropriate handling of the book, such as pulling at the head cap.

Text block: The text block of a book is made up of the signatures, or groups of pages, sewn together. It is the physical contents of the book. A text block can come loose from the case, the spine, or the hinges from age and mishandling.

BOOK REPAIR OVERVIEW

In this chapter the topic of material repairs will be covered. Because close to 80 percent of a library's collection is paper based, the focus will be on book repair. The treatment for nonprint media will also be discussed.

Anatomy of a Book

In the last chapter we talked about preventing damage to the spine by opening the book gently, having LSS gently pressing several pages against the front cover of the book, then doing the same to the pages in the back. This would continue until all of the pages have been pressed open so the book can lie flat. But we didn't talk about what the spine is, or any other part of a book, for that matter.

What we see when we look at a book is the front and back covers, a spine, and the pages inside. That is a little simplistic, as a typical hardcover book consists of many elements. First, there is the case, consisting of the front and back covers, or boards, and a stiff spine liner, or spine inlay, all covered by cloth or sturdy paper.

Then there is the text block, or the contents, which is made up of pages sewn or glued together: this is called a signature. A folded sheet of paper, or endpaper, is glued to the shoulder of the first and last page of the text block. The spine is lined with a cloth (or super) that extends onto the endpapers. It is then strengthened with a paper lining. This text block is attached to the case by gluing the endpaper and super to the boards. The spine is not glued to the lining of the text block; rather it creates a hollow that allows the book to easily open.

Finally, the hinge (or joint) takes the most strain of use and is usually the first area to show wear.[1]

Caring for Books

It may seem obvious, but to avoid book repair in the first place it is important to know how to care for a book. The first piece of advice was addressed previously— gently open the book to avoid cracking or breaking the spine. Most books for library or commercial use are made of paper and glue, so it is only common sense to realize that they are more fragile than not.

The lesson taught to children from the first day of school (and hopefully well before that) is to use clean hands. Dirt is difficult to remove and makes a book unattractive. As a matter of fact, books should be kept from babies and toddlers except for sturdy board or cloth books designed for that age group. Books should also be kept out of reach of pets as well (chewed books are virtually impossible to repair). Use bookmarks; don't read in the bathtub; and don't write in books—these are only a few of the basic commonsense rules that readers should follow.

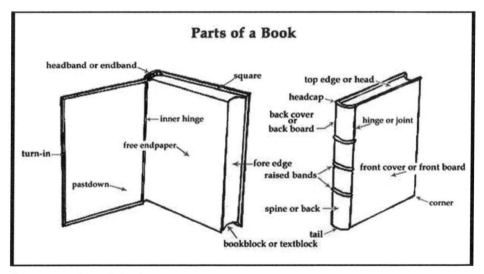

Figure 11.1. Parts of a book

TEXTBOX 11.1 HOW TO HANDLE A BOOK²

1. Have clean hands.
2. Use a bookmark—do not bend the corners of pages, or use objects like paper clips.
3. Close the book when you aren't reading, rather than leave it open face down. This can affect the spine.
4. Keep books away from pets.
5. Keep books away from babies and toddlers—given them cloth or board books.
6. Do not eat or drink when around books.
7. Use a photocopier rather than ripping out a page, but be careful not to mash the spine when you do.
8. Keep books dry: do not leave outdoors, do not read in the bathtub, and cover them when going from the library to the car.
9. Make notes—do not write, highlight, or underline in a book.
10. Do not attempt to make repairs yourself—it can cause more harm than good.

Other ways to unknowingly damage a book include letting them lean (without using a book end), which causes the spines to torque; shelving oversized books with the spines up (allowing the text block to loosen); and pulling books off the shelf by the head cap (which can rip the spine). Also, if LSS are displaying books they should use a book end or book stand specially made for that purpose. Nothing is sadder than seeing a shelf of books on display, leaning and slumping. Besides being unattractive, one can almost hear the spines breaking.

Some of the behaviors of well-meaning patrons that I have come across include writing grammatical corrections in a book, taping tears with cellophane tape, and in one instance, a patron disliked that her library book smelled of cigarette smoke, so she "helpfully" sprayed it with perfume before returning it.

Tools and Materials

There are tools and materials used for book repair, some as mundane as wax paper and knitting needles, and some specially designed for their acid-free and archival qualities. Library book repair supplies are available from a number of specialty companies as mentioned previously, such as Brodart, Demco, The Library Store, and University Products.

Tools that are used in book repair include:

- Bone folder: originally made of bone, they are now available in plastic. This is used to apply pressure when making creases on paper or pressing down glued surfaces. I have found this useful when covering books, to crease the plastic to fit the size of the book.
- Book press: this is used to apply pressure to a book's glued surface or other area that has been repaired. Although available commercially, bricks covered in brown paper or cloth work just as well.

- Brushes: available at hobby and art supply stores, brushes from one-half inch to one inch are good for applying glue.
- Knitting needles: these are used for tightening book hinges by inserting the glue-covered needle into the book hinge to get the glue all the way down.
- Ruler: a ruler is used to measure and mark materials to be cut—preferably a twelve-inch metal-edge ruler.
- Scissors: regular 8.5-inch scissors are good for almost anything that needs cutting. Smaller ones are useful as well.
- Waste paper strips are used to mask out an area so that adhesive can be applied exactly where needed.
- Wax paper: this is used to keep glued surfaces for a repaired book from sticking together. It is available from suppliers, although household wax paper is perfectly fine. Use your scissors to cut to size.
- X-Acto knives are good for scraping crayon from book covers, and for cutting.

Materials, or supplies, that are needed in book repair include:

- Archival-quality pressure tape: this is used to mend tears in paper but is acid free and thin.
- Binder tape is used to reattach broken hinges in heavy books. It is made of white cloth and is one and a half inches wide (other sizes are available). It has a line of stitching down the center.
- Book tape: this has a variety of uses, including reinforcement; it comes in a variety of colors and finishes; 2.5- to 3-inch widths are most common.
- Document cleaning pad: this is a cloth pad containing a nonabrasive powder that absorbs dirt from paper.
- Erasers: art gum or plastic erasers are used to remove pencil and ink marks.
- Hinge tape: this is used to reattach loose or broken hinges. Made of cloth, paper, or vinyl, it is usually white. One inch width is good.
- Liquid sticker remover: invaluable for removing sticky residue from book covers. It can also be bought locally without going through a supply catalog.
- PVA adhesive: this is also known as library glue. It is polyvinyl acetate, water based, and a strong vinyl resin that is quick drying, and dries clear.
- Sandpaper: sandpaper can be used to carefully remove marks from pages not affected by other cleaning methods. A fine grade is used.
- Wheat paste: this is a strong, non-deteriorating adhesive that blends into paper fibers and dries clear. It is available from library suppliers but can also be easily made in-house.

There are various other supplies that can be used by experienced menders, including heat-set tissue, silicone release paper, and Japanese paper, used for mending pages.[3]

PRINCIPLES OF REPAIR

When we talk about book repair there are a couple of options. If a book is badly damaged it may need professional repair or rebinding, but the majority of repairs

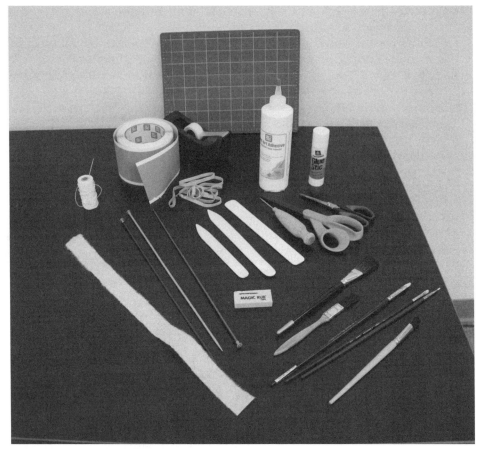

Figure 11.2.   Sample mending tools and materials. *S. Rosado*

that library books need are fairly minor and easily done in-house by LSS trained in basic book repair. This kind of repair is called "quick and dirty," and makes use of the tools and materials just discussed. Given the volume of books going in and out of a library, there will be a plentiful supply of books needing some kind of repair at any given time.

Book repair workshops are usually offered by local, regional, or state library agencies. While some suppliers offer free book repair pamphlets consisting of step-by-step directions, having the opportunity to take a hands-on repair class is worth the effort and cost.

There are three rules of repair:

Reversibility: Any treatment applied to a book should be reversible; that is it can be undone easily at a later date.

Do No Harm: This is a corollary to reversibility. If a repair seems difficult or you think you do not have the skills to complete the repair, set the book aside.

Expediency: Almost any non-brittle book can be repaired, given enough time and the proper equipment. Simple book repair implies that the repair will not take hours or days of staff time. As you become more comfortable with simple book repair, the decision to repair in-house versus sending the book to a commercial bindery will be easier to make.[4]

Marked and Torn Pages

Interestingly, when doing a Web search for "repairing marked pages," the first page of results was about fixing corrupt pages in Web documents and databases, or errors that cause automatic page-repair attempts. How far we've come!

It is to be expected that books that circulate will accumulate wear and tear, whether deliberate or not (as was mentioned earlier). Pencil marks are common, and they can be removed with an art gum or plastic eraser. When doing so, rub from the inner margin toward the edge. Rub gently, as paper can be wrinkled or torn. The above-mentioned document cleaning pad can also be used for any of the above. These pads contain a soft grit-free powder that absorbs and cleans surface dirt from paper, including dirt and smoke.

Ink is a little more difficult to remove. Some ink can be removed with an eraser, but if it isn't coming off easily, then move on to another source so the page doesn't get damaged. Unless the ink has penetrated the page, it may be possible to remove by gently scraping with an X-Acto knife. While this is feasible for fountain pen ink, ballpoint is almost impossible to remove. A steel eraser may help, but if it doesn't, it's best to just leave it alone. (This kind of damage should always be noted somewhere in the front of the book along with the date, to avoid blaming recent borrowers for something that may have been there for a long time.)

Crayon marks often shows up in children's books. A plastic eraser can remove the top layer, but it may be necessary to freeze the book to make the material brittle; the crayon mark can then be carefully scraped off. As distasteful as it may be, this method also works for gum and food that may have gotten onto the page.

The edges of a book can become dirty simply from repeated handling. Surprisingly, this can be cleaned up with fine-grade sandpaper gently rubbed over them. Wrap it around your fingers or a small block of wood to effectively get at the edges.

Torn pages may be easily repaired. There are several methods, depending on the severity of the tear. The easiest is simply to mend the tear with pressure-sensitive transparent tape. "The taping process is straightforward: First attach the tape just beyond the end of the tear and smooth it along the entire length of the tear. It's likely that the tear will extend to the edge of the page so it's best to cut the tape long enough that you can wrap about ½ inch of it over the edge to cover the other side of the tear. Don't try to trim the tape even with the edge of the page as you'll leave a rough edge that can snag and start a new tear."[5] Using a plastic or bone folder, run over the taped area to make sure it adheres. It is not necessary to tape the reverse side of the tear. As the tape may eventually collect dirt along the edges, be sure to only use it on books that are not valuable or part of a special collection.

Another method of repairing a tear, particularly if it is not a clean tear, is to use a liquid PVA adhesive. Put a piece of waxed paper underneath to avoid gluing the pages together. Gently apply a thin strip of glue, using a toothpick or small brush, to the torn edge. Overlap the torn edges carefully, especially if there is writing to match up. Rub lightly with a piece of cheesecloth, then put another piece of waxed paper over the repair. Smooth it out with the bone folder, and close the book with the waxed paper in place. Let it set for a couple of hours to overnight. When dry, gently pull off the waxed paper. It may stick a bit but should come off cleanly. Unlike tape, this tear will be virtually invisible.

For repairs to valuable or archival materials, it is best to repair using a wheat starch paste. This can be made at home with flour and deionized water according to very specific directions, both for the paste and the repair. Because it is more labor intensive and not likely to be needed for a circulating collection, this does not fall under the category of "quick and dirty." We'll leave this one for the preservationists.

Page Tip-ins

Sometimes a page comes completely free of the book. In this case it must be "tipped" in. The first step is placing sheets of waxed paper on both sides of the missing page. If the page was torn out and the edge is uneven, trim about an eighth

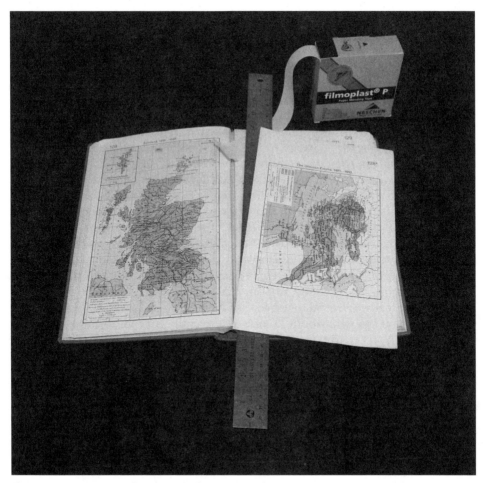

Figure 11.3. Tipping in a loose page with tape. *S. Rosado*

of an inch before you start. Then, apply a thin line of library adhesive to the edge with a small brush. Insert, or "tip in" the page so it lines up. Leaving the waxed paper in, close the book, wrap it tightly with several rubber bands (or use an H-Band made especially for this purpose), and put it under a book weight for several hours or overnight. When dry, carefully remove the waxed paper.

An alternative to using liquid PVA adhesive is to use special mending tape that is thin, transparent, and uses a slow-tacking adhesive that allows for moving the page into place and adjusting as needed.[6]

Cover Reattachment

Paperback books are the most likely to lose their covers, but reattaching them is not too difficult. First, make sure you scrape off any glue still attached to the book where it attached to the cover. If the book itself is falling apart, brush on a light coat of PVC adhesive to the text block and let it dry for several hours or overnight.

Take the detached cover and apply the adhesive to its spine (on the inside). Place the text block back into the cover, being sure to place a sheet of waxed paper in the front and back of the book where the spine meets the text block. Wrap securely with rubber bands (plentiful and cheap) or use a purchased H-band. Let it dry overnight; then remove the waxed paper. The next step is to reinforce the hinge using specially made hinge tape.

Hinges, Corners, and Spines

Hinges frequently come loose from the text block, or need reinforcing when the cover has been replaced. They can be repaired from within the book and from the outside. Use hinged book tape—made for this purpose it is split, or hinged, and has an adhesive back covered with paper. For the inside of a book to attach or reinforce a cover, cut the tape a quarter of an inch shorter than the book. Lifting the tape, remove the adhesive from one side and fold it around a ruler. Remove the other piece of paper from the adhesive, and gently lower the ruler into the space between the inside cover and the flyleaf—the hinge. Use the bone folder to press it into place and get maximum adhesion. Do the same for the other hinge.

Hinges can also be repaired with adhesive by applying it to where the text block and endpaper have separated. Using waxed paper, carefully brush PVA on the exposed spine lining and on the underside of the fold of the endpaper. Carefully align the endpaper and the text block to ensure that the fold of the end sheet exactly meets the shoulder of the text block. This will help to ensure proper opening of the book after drying. Use the bone folder to press the endpaper into the hinge. Make sure the waxed paper is in place, then close the book and use the bone folder to press gently on the outside of the hinge. Wrap with rubber bands and place the book in the book press overnight.

An even quicker method is to reinforce the hinge with hinge tape or simply clear or colored book tape. This is not always the most attractive way to do it, but it has its place. Textbooks and well-used but short-lived children's books may be candidates for this method.

Figure 11.4. Loose text block. *G. Keeler*

If a hinge is broken from the outside, it means the text block has come loose from the case. When you hold a book by the spine the gap can be very visible. In this case LSS can use the PVA adhesive and a knitting needle. Apply the glue along the length of the needle, and insert it into the gap created by the text block pulling away. Once the adhesive is applied, go back inside the book and use the bone folder to press it into place. Do the same on the other hinge; then rubber-band the book tightly and leave it, or place in the book press overnight.[7]

Hardbound books are usually protected by a book jacket. Cloth-covered books that are not and paperback books may need to have their corners protected. The library supply companies have specially made book corner tape that LSS may choose to use. It is shaped with "wings" for easy use, and all that needs to be done is to peel off the paper backing and place tape in the corner, fold over the wings, and it's done.

An alternative is to use two-inch book tape, carefully cut and folded around the corners. Yet another option for cloth-bound books is to put a little bit of PVA adhesive on a small brush, and paint it on the corners. Since it dries clear, there is no residue, and the corners are protected and prevented from further fraying.

Repairing or reinforcing spines takes a little more work. Clear book tape can be used on paperbacks; the size used will depend on the thickness of the book. Hardbound books are a little more difficult. If a hardback book spine merely needs reinforcing, then clear or colored book tape can be cut to size and placed carefully over the spine. If a spine needs replacing, then the LSS is in for a bigger job. The reason

TEXTBOX 11.2 SPINE TUBE REPAIR STEPS TO REATTACH HARD COVER TO TEXT

1. Make a hollow tube out of paper to glue into the spine of the book needing repair. Use heavyweight paper—about 70 lb. weight (not regular printer paper) for big heavy books, lighter-weight paper for lighter, smaller books.
2. Using a flexible tape measure, measure the height of the text block—*not* the book cover (e.g., 7¾ inches).
3. Measure the width of the text block at the rounded spine (e.g., 1½ inches).
4. Measure a rectangle and mark in pencil on your heavy-weight hollow tube paper. Height will be what you measured in #2 above, minus ½ inch (e.g., 7¾ inches – ½ inch = 7¼ inches tall—or a little bit shorter than height of text block).
5. Width of your rectangle will be three times the width measured in #3 above, minus ¼ inch (e.g., 1½ inches x 3 = 4½ inches – ¼ = 4¼ inches wide—or a little narrower than 3 times the width of the spine).
6. Cut out your rectangle.
7. Fold rectangle lengthwise the width you measured in #3 above (e.g., 1½ inches, and then do it again—or fold roughly into thirds—edges will not quite match up; that's OK).
8. After folding, glue section C down onto section A. When dry, you should be able to insert your finger into the "tube" of paper. Let dry before going to #9.
9. Glue tube to text block spine on one side (section C), and to back of book spine on the other side (back of section B). Rubber-band, press, and let dry.
10. Reinforce hinges inside with appropriate weight hinge tape.[8]

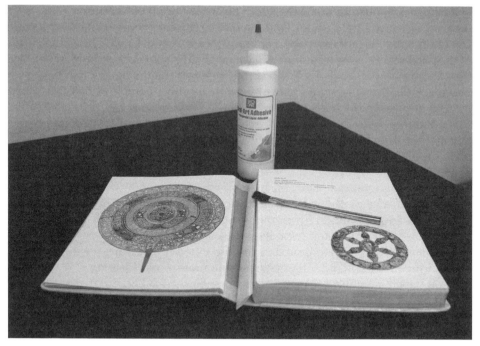

Figure 11.5. How to make a spine tube. *Courtesy of the author*

a spine would need to be replaced is if the hard cover became totally detached from the book, and the spine has to be rebuilt.

BINDERIES

Book binderies have a long and illustrious history:

> The art and business of bookbinding began with the protection of parchment manuscripts with boards. Papyrus had originally been produced in rolls, but sheets of parchment came to be folded and fastened together with sewing by the 2d century A.D. In the Middle Ages the practice of making fine bindings for these sewn volumes rose to great heights; books were rare and precious articles, and many were treated with exquisite bindings: they were gilded, jeweled, fashioned of ivory, wood, leather, or brass. The techniques of folding and sewing together sheets in small lots, combining those lots with tapes, and sewing and fastening boards on the outside as protection changed but little from the medieval monastery to the modern book bindery.[9]

Binderies today offer an array of services, from repair and restoration of existing books to binding of theses, manuscripts, periodicals, and business proposals. Some offer both glued and sewn bindings, as well as custom printing. There are times in libraries when repair is not possible and a book must be sent to a bindery for repair or rebinding. Often, new materials will come into the library with poor-quality

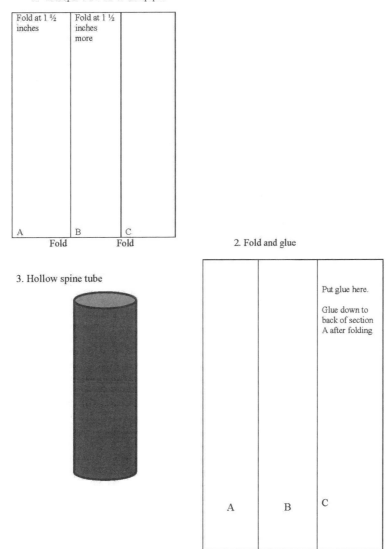

1. Example 4 1/2 x 7 ¼ inch paper

Fold at 1 ½ inches	Fold at 1 ½ inches more	
A	B	C
Fold	Fold	

2. Fold and glue

Put glue here.

Glue down to back of section A after folding

A   B   C

3. Hollow spine tube

Figure 11.6.   Spine tube repair with finished tube. *S. Rosado*

bindings, unsatisfactory soft covers, or poor paper. These factors all come under consideration when choosing to have a book rebound.

At the Bridgeport National Bindery in Agawam, MA, one can see the process from start to finish. Library books are rebound to extend shelf life; paperback books can be given hard covers for the same reason. Textbooks can be reprinted, manuscripts can be bound, and short runs can be printed in any quantity. While it looks like organized chaos, there is a distinct method for the procedure. Each order is numbered and matched to a central database that tracks its progress. They are routed from station to station for printing, cutting, gluing, and getting their covers. It is a strange

Figure 11.7. Books in process in a bindery. *Bridgeport National Bindery*

Figure 11.8. Print-on-demand equipment. *Bridgeport National Bindery*

mix of modern machinery and old-fashioned sewing machines. When finished the books are routed and packed for shipping.

Binderies are doing less rebinding than they once did due to the rise in popularity of e-books. Even downsized, the operation is impressive—and loud due to the machinery involved. To compensate for the loss of some of its operations, BNB has a separate room for print-on-demand (POD) books. Books sent in for rebinding or POD can range from a single volume (from a library or an individual) to a complete series of textbooks, for example. Turnaround for a POD can be as little as seventy-two hours.[10]

Costs are relatively low per item, and the overhead is passed on in the price to libraries and booksellers. Rebinding can be a cost-effective way to extend the life of heavily used items that are beyond the capabilities of the average book repair department. It can be the solution to preserving your family Bible but—as was stated previously—any work done to an item of value immediately devalues it.

NONBOOK MATERIAL

Nonbook material in libraries that can be quickly and easily repaired by LSS is limited to DVDs and CDs. They are both the same diameter and thickness, and are made up of layers of polycarbonate plastic. Small pits and bumps in the tracks encode the data. The key word here is "plastic"—thus they can, and do, become scratched, which affects their ability to be read, or played.[11]

The Web is full of suggestions for how to clean your CDs and DVDs using various materials such as banana peels, alcohol, toothpaste, baking soda, dishwashing soap, and car polish—and that is not the complete list! While not attesting to the efficacy of any of these home remedies, it is impractical to even think about doing this in a library that has hundreds of discs in the circulating collection.

LSS can, however, try a few simple things before resorting to more costly methods. First, hold the disc by the sides. Even if it is not scratched, dust, oils, and other contaminants may be present. LSS can use a soft brush to dust it, or run it under warm water for the same purpose. If there is stubborn dirt gently rub it while wet—adding a liquid soap can help. Or use alcohol with a cotton swab, and rub outward from the center. Do not dry the disc with a cloth—rather, let it air dry. Try to play it again.[12] If this doesn't work, then it's the disc cleaning machine to the rescue.

For very large collections it may be recommended that the library invest in a heavy-duty disc repair machine. As technology changes constantly, so do disc cleaning machines, so it's a good idea to check with other libraries of similar size to see what they are using. Large heavy-duty machines can cost hundreds or even thousands of dollars, but considering the size of a given collection, it may be well worth the investment. A large collection may also have more significant wear and tear on CDs, DVDs, Blu-Ray, and gaming discs. There are also smaller disc repair machines on the market that are readily available and affordable, with price tags under $50. While many of them are marketed for the consumer, they are being used by libraries with good results. They come with solutions or sprays that clean and recondition while smoothing out light surface scratches that can cause a disc to skip, freeze, or simply not play. They renew the disc's protective layer without affecting the data.

Other nonbook materials, such as magazines, pamphlets, and maps, would be treated as paper-based books using the same, or similar, repair methods. The companies mentioned previously, such as Brodart and Demco, offer pamphlets and guides to book repair; additionally Demco currently offers online book repair how-to videos.[13] A search of the Web and YouTube will return dozens of online tutorials that bring to life that which we have been discussing in this chapter.

CHAPTER SUMMARY

In this chapter we have covered the basics of book repair that LSS could accomplish in a library. These are generally "quick and dirty" repairs that can be done with a minimum of effort, but with care and skill to get the materials back on the shelf. The tools and materials were introduced as well as specific examples of how to make repairs, from cleaning to repairing tears, hinges, and spines. While only an introduction, as book repair can get very complicated, it is a starting point for LSS who need to perform in-house book repairs.

DISCUSSION QUESTIONS

1. What are the parts of a book, and what can go wrong with them?
2. What is meant by "quick and dirty" repair?
3. Describe some of the tools used for book repair, and explain how they are used.
4. What are the three rules of repair?
5. Describe a nonbook item, and how it can be repaired.

ACTIVITIES

1. Make arrangements with the technical services department of a library of your choice to observe LSS in the process of performing repairs on damaged books. Write a one-page essay of your experience.
2. Based on what you have read and observed, in person or on the Web, try it yourself: take a discarded book and remove its cover, tear some pages, or break the hinges. Using the proper tools and materials, repair the damage. (If you do not work in a library, you will need to make arrangements with the technical services department of a library for permission to use their supplies.)

NOTES

1. *An Introduction to Book Repair* (Syracuse, NY: Gaylord, 1998), 2–3.
2. George M. Eberhart, *The Whole Library Handbook 3* (Chicago, IL: American Library Association, 2000), 345.
3. *Book Repair: Supplies and Tools*, photograph, Smith Library, Eastern CT State University, November 24, 2015, accessed March 4, 2016.

4. "A Simple Book Repair: Guiding Principles," Dartmouth College Library, last modified January 1, 2012, accessed March 1, 2016, http://www.dartmouth.edu/~library/preservation/repair/guideprinc.html?mswitch-redir=classic.

5. John Ison, "The Book Doctor Is In: Book Repair ASAP," Ideas + Inspiration from Demco (blog), last modified June 23, 2015, accessed March 3, 2016, http://ideas.demco.com/blog/book-repair-series-2/.

6. *Book Repair: Tipping in Pages*, photograph, Smith Library, Eastern CT State University, November 24, 2015, accessed March 4, 2016.

7. Peter D. Verheyen and Marianne Hanley, "Book Repair Basics for Libraries," Association for Library Collections & Technical Services (ALCTS), accessed March 3, 2016, http://downloads.alcts.ala.org/ce/091411book_repair_basics.pdf.

8. *Book Repair: Spine Repair with Hollow Tube*, photograph, Smith Library, Eastern CT State University, November 24, 2015, accessed March 4, 2016.

9. "Bookbinding," in *Columbia Electronic Encyclopedia*, 6th ed. (New York: Columbia University Press, 2015).

10. Brian Baird, interview. Bridgeport National Bindery, Agawam, MA. December 15, 2015.

11. Gayle A. Alleman, "How DVDs Work," How Stuff Works: Tech, last modified 2016, accessed March 4, 2016, http://electronics.howstuffworks.com/dvd2.htm.

12. "How to Fix a Scratched CD," WikiHow, accessed March 4, 2016, http://www.wikihow.com/Fix-a-Scratched-CD.

13. "Library Collection Care Videos," YouTube, last modified December 11, 2013, accessed March 4, 2016, https://www.youtube.com/playlist?list=PL9876A71BE2C6220C.

REFERENCES, SUGGESTED READINGS, AND WEBSITES

Alleman, Gayle A. "How DVDs Work." How Stuff Works: Tech. Last modified 2016. Accessed March 4, 2016. http://electronics.howstuffworks.com/dvd2.htm.

Baird, Brian. Interview. Bridgeport National Bindery, Agawam, MA. December 15, 2015.

"Bookbinding." In *Columbia Electronic Encyclopedia*. 6th ed. New York, Columbia University Press, 2015.

Book Repair: Spine Repair with Hollow Tube. Photograph. Smith Library, Eastern CT State University. November 24, 2015. Accessed March 4, 2016.

Book Repair: Supplies and Tools. Photograph. Smith Library, Eastern CT State University. November 24, 2015. Accessed March 4, 2016.

Book Repair: Tipping in Pages. Photograph. Smith Library, Eastern CT State University. November 24, 2015. Accessed March 4, 2016.

Brodart Co. "Library Supplies: Book Care and Repair." Brodart. Accessed March 4, 2016. http://www.shopbrodart.com/library-supplies-school-supplies/book-care/?=.

Dartmouth College. "A Simple Book Repair Manual: Parts of a Book." Dartmouth College Library. Last modified January 5, 2012. Accessed May 19, 2016. http://www.dartmouth.edu/~library/preservation/repair/bookparts.html.

Dartmouth College. "A Simple Book Repair: Guiding Principles." Dartmouth College Library. Last modified January 1, 2012. Accessed March 1, 2016. http://www.dartmouth.edu/~library/preservation/repair/guideprinc.html?mswitch-redir=classic.

Demco. "Library Supplies: Book Repair." Demco. Accessed March 4, 2016. http://demco.com/goto?PNHC68&intcmp=CN_C68.

Eberhart, George M. *The Whole Library Handbook 3*. Chicago, IL: American Library Association, 2000.

An Introduction to Book Repair. Syracuse, NY: Gaylord, 1998.

Ison, John. "The Book Doctor Is In: Book Repair ASAP." Ideas + Inspiration from Demco. Last modified June 23, 2015. Accessed March 3, 2016. http://ideas.demco.com/blog/book-repair-series-2/.

Verheyen, Peter D., and Marianne Hanley. "Book Repair Basics For Libraries." Association for Library Collections & Technical Services (ALCTS). Accessed March 3, 2016. http://downloads.alcts.ala.org/ce/091411book_repair_basics.pdf.

WikiHow. "How to Fix a Scratched CD." WikiHow. Accessed March 4, 2016. http://www.wikihow.com/Fix-a-Scratched-CD.

YouTube. "AbeBooks Explains the Parts of a Book." YouTube. Last modified September 28, 2011. Accessed March 4, 2016. https://www.youtube.com/watch?v=DQyntYcGwik.

———. "Library Collection Care Videos." YouTube. Last modified December 11, 2013. Accessed March 4, 2016. https://www.youtube.com/playlist?list=PL9876A71BE2C6220C.

Glossary

Academic library: Academic libraries serve society's need for education for those beyond high school, including community colleges, four-year colleges, and universities. Their collections serve the students and faculty of the institution. These libraries serve the teaching needs of the institution as well as those of the students. They may also support faculty research.

Acquisitions: Acquisitions is the function of collections that concerns ordering and receiving print and nonprint materials. Specifically the acquisitions department, or the LSS who work in acquisitions, uses evaluative sources to find and verify that an item exists, chooses a vendor, places the order, maintains a fiscal record, and receives the materials.

Acquisitions: The acquisition of materials in a library means ordering and receiving print and nonprint materials. It does not refer to the selection of these materials, nor does it refer to the ordering of office supplies or library equipment. The former is done by collection development or selection staff; the latter by the business or technical services department.

AENGLC rank: AENGLC rank means the adjusted equalized net grand list per capita, a measure of town wealth calculated annually. The lower the number is, the wealthier the town. This is an important factor when comparing libraries in different parts of the state. While helpful, it is only used in Connecticut.

ALA-LSSC: American Library Association-Library Support Staff Certification, a national certification program designed to allow library support staff to demonstrate their competencies.

American Library Association: ALA is a national organization that provides leadership and information services to the library profession.

Barcodes: Barcodes are a machine-readable code in the form of numbers and a pattern of parallel lines of varying width. The first six numbers of the barcode are the publisher's country and identification number; the next five digits represent the book's number. The last number is called a check digit, which enables the scanner to determine if the barcode was scanned correctly. They are used in libraries to identify items and patrons.

Bindery: A book bindery is a facility that rebinds, repairs, and produces print books. Rebinding a book means replacing a damaged cover with a new one, either by reusing the original artwork or making a new plain cover. A bindery can also add hard covers to paperback books. They usually have the capability of creating a book from scratch, as well as providing print-on-demand services.

Bone folder: Bone folders, originally made of bone, are now available in plastic. They are usually white, oblong, and come in several sizes—usually six to seven inches long, an inch or so wide, and three-quarters of an inch thick. The edges are rounded. They are used to apply pressure when making creases on paper or pressing down glued surfaces.

Branding: Branding is the process involved in creating a unique name and image for a product in the consumer's mind, through advertising campaigns with a consistent theme. This is an effective tool to promote the library's collection.

Budgets: A budget is an estimate of income and expenses over a defined period of time—usually the library's fiscal year. It is critical for libraries to keep a budget in order to determine where funds are needed for allocation, and the source from which they will come.

Cataloging: Cataloging means creating a bibliographic record of an item. In addition we use numerical or alphabetical classification systems to organize materials by subject. These systems provide for the arrangement of materials on a shelf or in a database in logical order, making it easy for patrons to find that for which they are searching. This is an important factor in creating collections.

Collection: A collection can have many meanings but is usually thought of as a group of objects or materials accumulated in one place, usually for some purpose. In the library setting it is an accumulation of information resources in multiple formats, usually developed by library professionals for a particular group of users. These materials are usually connected to each other in some way as well as connected to an intended audience, or user.

Collection development: Collection development refers to the process of building a library collection in a variety of formats to serve recreational, study, teaching, research, and other needs of library users. The process includes selection and deselection of materials, the planning of strategies for continuing acquisition, and evaluation of collections to determine how well they serve user needs. It includes library operations ranging from the selection of individual titles for purchase, to the withdrawal of expendable materials.

Collection development policies: A collection policy, also known as a selection policy, is a document that provides guidance for the librarians or LSS who do collection development. It follows a set of guidelines to consider when choosing materials, and includes such criteria as positive reviews, reputation of the author, local interest, demand, and budget limitations.

Collection promotion: Collection promotion is the activity that LSS perform to advertise or highlight what the library has to offer in their print and digital collections. It can be done in-house with displays and promotions, or through outreach to traditional and social media.

Collection reports: A collection report is run on an automated library system to provide statistical information of the items in a particular collection, such as the monthly circulation of children's books. It provides a snapshot of the activity of that area.

Collection shifting: Collection shifting is an ongoing task to perform to avoid shelves getting too tight—that is, having so many books jammed in that it is often impossible to pull a single item off the shelf. It makes the shelves more attractive and promotes use of the collection.

Common Core standards: The Common Core is a set of high-quality academic standards in mathematics and English Language Arts/Literacy (ELA) that help determine what a student should know and be able to do at the end of each grade. It impacts libraries and changes the way traditional library skills are being taught; it also encourages a close collaboration between school and public librarians.

Community assessment: Community assessment is the analysis of the demographics of a community. Statistical data provide a good place to start to determine the population, age range, genders, and ethnicities of a particular area, as well as employers, types of households, age, number of schools and libraries, social service providers, languages spoken, and median family incomes.

Conservation: Conservation is a specific term used in the field of preservation that refers to the physical care given to individual items within collections. This ranges from the repair of circulating collections to the restoration of rare materials. This should only be done by recognized conservators from certified programs.

CREW: CREW stands for Continuous Revision Evaluation Weeding. First created in 1976, it is a method that provides guidelines for evaluating, and ultimately deselecting, materials from a library collection. It is a manual that has been updated and expanded to keep pace with modern standards and technology.

Databases: A database is basically an electronic index or catalog. It contains an organized collection of information that allows users to search for a particular topic, article, or book. One that we are most familiar with is the library's OPAC, which is itself a database that allows users to search for resources in a library.

DDA/PDA/UDA: Demand-driven acquisition and patron-driven acquisition, also known as user-driven acquisition, is a method that allows patrons to contribute to the acquisition of materials for library collection through an electronic program in the user's catalog.

Demographics: Demographics are the statistics of a given population by age, sex, race, and income. This is important for libraries so they can know whom they are serving, and for whom they can provide the appropriate resources. This is a key component of community assessment and subsequently, collection development.

Deselection: Deselection, also known as weeding, means to cull, or withdraw from the collection, materials that are outdated and no longer useful. The justification for deselection is to maintain a collection that is vital, relevant, and useful. It should be a part of an overall collection development policy and is a continuous process.

Digital materials: Digital materials are those that are not in print or book form. In a library they can consist of research databases, electronic serials or journals, electronic books, audiobooks, and streaming content. They are an important element of a library collection but may have issues of access and cost.

Digitization: Digitization is the process of converting materials to a digital, or electronic, format. Digitizing books is already available in the form of e-books from commercial publishers; it can be considered a form of preservation in that once a book, image, or document is converted to this format it may be used to replace the more fragile paper-based original.

Disaster planning: Disaster planning means creating a working plan for how the library would respond in the event of a severe emergency, such as weather-related issues, fire, and water damage. It includes having an emergency kit of supplies and a list of contacts, and it addresses prevention as well as remediation.

Discovery Systems: Discovery systems, also called Web-scale discovery, means using an interface directed toward the library users to find materials in its collection, and subsequently to gain access to items of interest through the appropriate mechanisms. Discovery products tend to be independent from the specific applications that libraries use to manage resources, such as an ILS or electronic resources management systems.

Expediency: Expediency means that almost any non-brittle book can be repaired, given enough time and the proper equipment. Simple book repair implies that the repair will not take hours or days of staff time.

Freedom to Read Statement: The Freedom to Read Statement is a document created by the American Library Association (ALA, the national professional library association) to affirm that libraries make available the widest diversity of views and expressions.

Funding: Funding is the means by which libraries pay the bills. Most school and public libraries are financially supported by their local municipality; academic library funding will depend on whether it's a public or private institution. Public libraries in particular depend also on grants, donations, or fund-raising drives to augment their funds.

Government information: Government information may also be referred to as public information. It is defined as information created, compiled, and/or maintained by the federal government that is owned by the people, held in trust by the government, and should be available to all.

Hinges: Hinges are the portion of the book closest to the spine that allows the book to be opened and closed. When a book is dropped or otherwise stressed, the hinges can come loose or even be broken. This can also happen from age as glue dries out. They need to be repaired to hold the book together.

HVAC: HVAC refers to a heating, ventilation, and air-conditioning system. It controls the temperature and humidity of a building to maintain a constant rate. This is an environment critical to paper-based collections and should be in all libraries.

Integrated library systems: An integrated library system, or ILS, is a computer system and programs that link library operations. It consists of components, or modules, that do different tasks. These modules are for acquisitions, cataloging, serials, and circulating materials.

Inventory: An inventory is a complete listing of the items in a collection. Physically inventorying a library collection means that every item in the collection will be examined to assess its status, including its placement on the shelf, its cataloging, and its use or circulation activity.

ISBN: The ISBN is the International Standard Book Number, a unique thirteen-digit number assigned to each edition of a work. The same title published in regular text, large print, or on CD will each have a different ISBN. It is the most reliable method of verification. The ISBN is divided into elements representing prefix, country, publisher, format, and check digit.

Item reports: Item reports are those run by an automated system that are specific to a particular item or category, such as all items in a certain Dewey number, or all DVDs that the library owns. Item reports are an important part of evaluating a collection.

Library Bill of Rights: The Library Bill of Rights is a document created by the American Library Association (ALA, the national professional library association), affirming basic policies that guide library service. It is based on the principles of the U.S. Constitution and guides librarians in providing equal service to all patrons.

LSS: Library Support Staff as defined by ALA-LSSC.

Marketing: Marketing is the process of promoting a service to a target audience. Libraries routinely market collections, services, and programs to bring users into the library to increase their use.

Mission: An organization's mission identifies its value and purpose to the community it serves. It explains what the organization is, and what functions it serves. By establishing a mission, usually in a "mission statement," an organization or library can develop and provide the services that meet the needs of their constituents.

Needs assessment: A needs assessment is a systematic process for determining and addressing *needs*, or "gaps," between current conditions and desired "wants." The discrepancy between the current condition and wanted condition must be measured to appropriately identify the need.

Networks: A network is a way to share applications or information between two or more workstations for the purpose of sharing information. It may be as small as two computers networked to share one printer, and as large as libraries networked to form a consortium. In a typical library there may be several workstations connected to each other in one building.

Nonprint materials: Nonprint, or nonbook items, are those that are not paper based and include electronic books, full-text serial databases, electronic newspapers, and media such as CDs, DVDs, Blu-Ray, and Playaways. These materials represent a large part of a library's collection, and their selection is evaluated in several different ways.

Open-source software: Open-source software allows libraries to get licensed use of the source code to modify or manipulate their ILS to suit their individual library needs. OSS is usually created by a collaborative group of individuals who then distribute the source code to programmers, who can alter it as needed.

Outsourcing: Outsourcing is another way that libraries can acquire materials by contracting with a service that does the selection and processing without input from the staff. This takes the entire acquisition function out of the library.

Physical processing: Physical processing means that any item a library receives must be prepared to circulate. It includes affixing barcodes, spine labels, reader interest labels, book covers, jewel cases, and so on, so the item can be both identified and protected.

Preparation: Preparation means making print and nonprint items ready for use, such as the physical processing of items. The LSS must use methods to establish ownership of the library's materials and to provide for their tracking once they go into the collection.

Preservation: Preservation is a term in general use to define activities that will prolong the life of materials by particular attention to solutions concerning entire collections. It includes concerns about the environment, handling, and storage. This can be done by staff trained in a few basic concepts.

Print-on-demand services (POD): POD is a service that allows books to be printed one at a time as needed. Binderies offer this service, as do a number of online services. A bindery can produce one, or a series of books in any quantity, using the POD machine.

Programming: Programming is the offering of events, classes, lectures, and so on, to the variety of library patrons in any given community. It serves to bring people to the library as well as create community spirit. Keeping statistics on library programs is valuable when evaluating library services.

Proprietary software: Proprietary software consists of computer programs that are the exclusive property of their developers or publishers, and cannot be copied or distributed without complying with their licensing agreements. Many integrated library systems use proprietary software.

Public library: The public library serves a culturally diverse population and a variety of ages, and is the most heterogeneous of any type of library. Public service then is structured around these populations to best serve their particular demographic. They are places of cultural preservation of information in its various formats and are often the hub of their community.

Publishers: A publisher taps the sources of material, usually through agents and editors. Raises and supplies the capital, or funds, to run the publishing operation that aids in the development of the material, provides for the legal work necessary, distributes and promotes the material, and maintains the records of the organization.

PVA: PVA stands for polyvinyl acetate, a water-based, pH-neutral, and acid-free adhesive. It is white but dries clear and quickly. PVA is the standard in library glue for repairs and binding.

QR code: A QR code is the abbreviation of Quick Response code and is the trademark for a type of barcode. It has greater readability and storage capacity compared to standard UPC barcodes. QR codes consist of black modules (square dots) arranged in a square grid on a white background, which can be read by an imaging device (such as a camera or scanner).

Quick and dirty repair: "Quick and dirty" repairs are those that can be done with a minimum of effort, but with care and skill to get the materials back on the shelf. They include cleaning pages, mending tears, and fixing loose hinges.

Repair: Repair is the physical treatment carried out upon circulation collections to prolong their usable life. It includes repairing covers, mending pages and bindings, and cleaning pages. This can be done by anyone trained in the correct methods.

Resource sharing: Resource sharing is libraries collaborating with one another to maximize access by sharing their collections. This is done through interlibrary loan, integrated library systems, and shared databases.

Reversibility: Reversibility is the principle that a treatment applied to a book should be reversible—that is, it can be undone easily at a later date. Treatments would be undone if newer or better repairs can be performed or if the book is of significant value (as repairs lower the value).

RFID: RFID, or radio-frequency identification, is a method that combines microchips and radio technology to track items. Installed in library material, it allows the library to find an item in the building; when used for checking out materials, it can track the location of that item within its range.

RH: RH stands for relative humidity. Humidity is the water vapor in the air. It is directly related to temperature and should be at about a 45 percent level in a library at all times. Too much fluctuation in either direction can damage paper and paper-based materials.

School library/media center: School libraries, or media centers, have evolved from a simple collection of books into a resource center of media and technology; their collections reflect the demographics of the student body. The media specialist or LSS provide library instruction and work with teachers to coordinate lesson plans and materials for classroom support.

Security strips: Security strips are magnetized strips embedded in adhesive tape that are affixed between the pages, or spine and binding, of a book. If they leave the building without being desensitized they will set off the alarm of a special gate at the exit. Once they are desensitized, they can leave; upon check-in they must be resensitized.

Selection (1): Selection means choosing the materials that a library will purchase using such tools as review journals, online programs, electronic databases, vendors, and "best lists." Selection must take into account the demographics of the library's community as well as the funds available.

Selection (2): The selection of materials for inclusion in a library follows a set of criteria, often found in a library collection development policy. Criteria include, but are not limited to, the reputation of the author, authoritativeness, literary style, timeliness of subject, read-ability, and format.

Serials: "Serials" is an all-inclusive term covering a variety of publications of various forms, content, and purpose, such as magazines and newspapers. They are issued in successive parts, at regular intervals, and are intended to continue indefinitely.

Shelf list: The term "shelf list" refers to the practice of having a master list of every item in the library held apart from the regular catalog. It is used to compare library holdings to actual items. Previously done with catalog cards, most shelf lists are now held electronically in a database.

Shelf reading: Shelf reading describes the process of physically going along a row of books to make sure they are in the correct order, either alphabetically or by call number. This en-sures that items are where they are supposed to be in order to be easily located.

Shifting: Collection shifting is an ongoing task to perform to avoid shelves getting too tight—that is, having so many books jammed in that it is often impossible to pull a single item off the shelf. This creates a more inviting look and enables the browser to find materials more easily.

Spine: The spine of a book is its backbone. It is attached to the front and back covers to form the case for the text block to fit into. If the spine is broken or pulls away, the entire book can fall apart. Spines can also be damaged by inappropriate handling of the book, such as pulling at the head cap.

Statistics: Statistics is the practice dealing with the collection, analysis, interpretation, and presentation of large quantities of numerical data. It is a useful tool for libraries to evaluate their collections and services.

Storage: Storage, an integral part of collection management, includes the routine and ap-propriate shelving of materials according to their format. It also involves shelf reading to determine that the collection is in order; collection shifting, to accommodate addition or withdrawal of materials; and print and digital management.

Text block: The text block of a book is made up of the signatures, or groups of pages, sewn together. It is the physical contents of the book. A text block can come loose from the case, the spine, or the hinges from age and mishandling.

UPC: UPC, or Universal Product Code, is a specific kind of barcode that is used for products other than library materials, such as in stores. UPC is a linear barcode made up of two parts: the barcode and the twelve-digit UPC number. The first six numbers of the barcode are the manufacturer's identification number. The next five digits represent the item's number.

Vendors: Vendors, also known as jobbers or wholesalers, are a third party that buys print and nonprint materials from publishers to resell to public, school, and academic libraries at a discount. They provide the advantage of "one stop shopping"—they can supply materials from a variety of publishers.

Verification: Confirmation that the bibliographic information of an item is accurate. This is done to be sure that the item actually exists, and to determine if it is needed for the col-lection. It is also needed to determine if the bibliographic data provided is correct. This ensures that the correct item in the correct format is chosen for the collection.

Index

Page references for figures are italicized.

About the Author

Hali R. Keeler has been an adjunct professor since 1998 in the Library Technology Program at Three Rivers Community College in Norwich, Connecticut, where she formerly served as program coordinator. She teaches library public services, library technical services, and management strategies. Hali earned her MLS from the University of Rhode Island and has an MA in French. Retired after thirty-five years in public library service as a children's librarian and a library director, she has been a longtime member of the American Library Association (ALA), Public Library Association (PLA), and the Connecticut Library Association (CLA). Offices she has held include chair of the Public Libraries Section of CLA, trustee of CLA, and president of the Southeastern CT Library Association. She is the author of "Library Technology Program: Three Rivers Community College," *Library Mosaics: The Magazine for Support Staff* 16, no. 1 (January/February 2005): 12; and *Foundations of Library Service*, Library Support Staff Handbooks 1 (Lanham, MD: Rowman & Littlefield, 2015).